PURE & SIMPLE

HOMEMADE INDIAN VEGETARIAN CUISINE

First paperback edition published in 2012 by
Interlink Books
An imprint of Interlink Publishing Group, Inc.
46 Crosby Street, Northampton, Massachusetts 01060
www.interlinkbooks.com

ISBN: 978-1-56656-881-4

Text and photography © Vidhu Mittal

Editor: Neeta Datta
American edition editors: Hiltrud Schulz, Sara Rauch, Leyla Moushabeck
Design: Supriya Saran
American edition cover design: Juliana Spear
Production: Naresh Nigam

Printed and bound in India

To request our free 40-page full-color catalog, please call us toll free at
1-800-238-LINK; visit our website at www.interlinkbooks.com,
or send us an email: info@interlinkbooks.com

PURE & SIMPLE

HOMEMADE INDIAN VEGETARIAN CUISINE

VIDHU MITTAL

Photography by
SANJAY RAMCHANDRAN

Interlink Books

An imprint of Interlink Publishing Group, Inc.
Northampton, Massachusetts

For every vegetarian food lover

ACKNOWLEDGEMENTS

Sanjay Ramchandran who very patiently took photographs. His creativity reflects in this book.

Jagdish Babu DK who systematically rearranged selected photographs and text. It was a boon for a non-tech savvy person like me to have him around.

Sujatha Puranik Rakhra, an invaluable sounding board, who was always there for me whenever I needed her.

Abhishek Poddar, who has a creative eye, gave several ideas for the layout and the cover page.

William GK who assisted in the final styling of each dish before it was shot.

And, most importantly, my husband, **Som**, our children, **Nidhi**, **Tarang**, and **Siddharth**, my sister, **Anu**, and my domestic help, **Madamma**, who supported me as I journeyed through this book.

CONTENTS

FOREWORD

Even before our father's job took us to Bangalore, our parents were great hosts. They loved having friends and family over for vivacious gatherings. Aside from the great company, the hallmark of these events was, undeniably, food.

The spreads were highlighted with Indian classics like *dal makhani* and *methi paneer,* as well as continental gems like corn with spinach, casseroles, and potato with mixed vegetable cakes.

As our parents' social circle grew larger and more eclectic, so did the opportunity for the two of them to hone their entertaining skills.

It was during this time that a close friend of our mother's, and a regular at these gatherings, encouraged her to consider sharing her culinary skills. Our family jumped onboard, making posters for "Fancy Chef Cookery Classes."

Her first course – Party Cooking – spanned five days, during the work week, and had two simple tenets: vegetarianism and delighting a crowd. For three hours every day, our dining room was transformed into a working kitchen, complete with a portable stove, notebooks, and raw ingredients. Five housewives made up the first class. My mother's tasty, yet easy-to-prepare recipes, along with her straightforward teaching style lead to all five returning for the sequel: Party Cooking 2.

With these humble beginnings in culinary pedagogy, Mom expanded her selection of classes to include international cuisine. When dining at the newest eatery in Bangalore, she always tried to figure out how to recreate the dishes. And then we'd return home to be guinea pigs for her experiments.

Nobody ever heard the two of us complain. For sixteen years, we have watched her make many aspiring cooks (and as a consequence, their families) very happy. This book is a culmination of what she's learned and is sure to spread that joy to many more.

Nidhi and Tarang

INTRODUCTION

Around the globe, popularity in both Indian cuisine and vegetarianism is rising steadily. This book will introduce you to the joys of cooking and even show how it can actually be a relaxing activity. Arming you with simple methods, this book will allow you to recreate the intricate flavors, intoxicating aromas, and succulent textures of homestyle Indian food.

I have been conducting cookery classes in Bangalore, India, for over 15 years and it has been one of my most rewarding experiences. My many students have been the source of encouragement and inspiration for writing this book.

The recipes in this book have the characteristic flavor of my native province – Uttar Pradesh. My emphasis has been on crafting delicately spiced dishes, contrary to the hot flavors stereotypically associated with Indian cuisine.

Combinations of these recipes make for delicious menus that are also very well-balanced meals. You will find many ways to pick and choose various courses like soups, salads, refreshing drinks, entrées, and scrumptious desserts.

I have had the opportunity to perfect these recipes over the years. With these dishes, I have also tried to illustrate the immense visual appeal of Indian food and highlight the natural colors of the freshest ingredients. The preparations for these recipes involve very simple and easy-to-understand steps. Photographs accompany all the recipes and highlight each step of the process.

I hope you and your loved ones enjoy cooking these dishes as much as I have enjoyed writing this book.

Vidhu Mittal

DISCOVER SPICES

Spices are essential food additives enhancing the flavor, aroma, and also color of the food. These are natural and dried and used either whole or ground. Some of these can be sprinkled but the true flavors are enhanced when roasted, preheated in a cooking medium, or added during cooking. Spices must be stored in airtight containers to retain freshness.

 **Asafetida** (*hing*): It is a resin from a tree and has a strong smell when raw, but when cooked it imparts a smooth flavor. This spice aides in digestion and is used in food as a condiment. It must be stored away from other spices because of its strong odor.

 Bay leaf (*tej patta*): It is a dried leaf of the bay laurel tree, and has a pleasant flavor. Normally a dish is seasoned with 2-3 leaves. The fragrance of bay leaf is more obvious than the taste in cooked food. Leaves can be removed before serving.

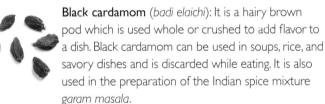 **Black cardamom** (*badi elaichi*): It is a hairy brown pod which is used whole or crushed to add flavor to a dish. Black cardamom can be used in soups, rice, and savory dishes and is discarded while eating. It is also used in the preparation of the Indian spice mixture *garam masala*.

 Black peppercorn (*sabut kali mirch*): It is a sun-dried berry of a pepper plant. Black peppercorn is sometimes used whole, but is more often ground. It is also the main ingredient in the Indian spice mixture called *garam masala*.

 Black salt (*kala namak*): It is an unrefined mineral salt, greyish in color. It is used extensively in Indian cooking as it enhances the flavor in *chaats* and savories.

 Carom (*ajwain*) **seeds**: Carom seeds are greyish brown in color; they are aromatic and slightly pungent in taste. Only a small quantity added to clarified butter (*ghee*) or oil is enough to flavor the dish. This helps reduce flatulence.

 Chili powder (*lal mirch*): It is a hot spice prepared from ground red chilies and the spiciness varies with the type of chili used. Small quantity of chili powder is added to oil while cooking curries. It can also be sprinkled over *chaat* and *raita* to add an extra zing. Kashmiri red chilies are often used as they add color and are less spicy.

 Cinnamon (*dalchini*): This is a bark of a tree, which is rolled and then dried. Cinnamon has an aromatic and sweet flavor. Ground cinnamon is widely used in soups, desserts, and stews. Cinnamon sticks are used for indirect flavoring in a dish and may be removed while eating.

 Clove (*laung*): It is an aromatic dried flower bud. It is used for both sweet and savory dishes. Rice and soups seasoned with cloves in ghee or oil infuse a soothing flavor.

 Coriander (*dhaniya*) **seeds**: These are dried fruits of the cilantro plant, greenish brown in color with a slight savory flavor. Ground coriander is widely used in Indian curries.

 Cumin (*jeera*) **seeds**: These are small, elongated seeds which have a distinctive aroma and flavor. Cumin seeds emit their own flavor after browning in oil for curries. They can also be roasted and ground and are used for flavoring yogurt dishes.

 Fennel (*saunf*) **seeds**: These are small, elongated, aromatic, and light green in color. They have a sweet taste. Ground fennel seeds are used in curries and pickles. Whole seeds are often chewed in India as a mouth freshener.

 Fenugreek seeds (*methi dana*): These are hard and pale yellow in color with a bitter taste. Only a few seeds are added for seasoning and flavoring. Ground or whole seeds are used in Indian pickles and emit a pleasant aroma.

Green cardamom (*choti elaichi*): These are light green in color with tiny, black seeds inside. The cardamom seeds are groundd and used in sweet dishes, tea, and some exotic dishes. Green cardamom has a distinctive, refreshing flavor and is also a good mouth freshener.

Jaggery (*gur*): This is boiled and solidified raw sugarcane juice, used extensively in Indian cooking. It has a unique flavor and is used in both sweet and savory dishes. It is considered healthier than sugar as it retains more mineral salts.

Mango powder (*amchur*): This is the sun-dried powdered form of raw mangoes. It is generally added to cooking vegetables toward the end to give a tangy flavor to the dish. Adding earlier can delay the cooking process.

Mint (*pudina*) **powder**: This is the sun-dried powdered form of fragrant mint leaves. It adds a refreshing flavor to drinks, dry vegetables, Indian breads, and curries. Mint powder can be stored for up to a month.

Mustard seeds (*rai*): These are the small, round seeds of the mustard plant. The color varies from black to brown to yellow. Savory dishes are tempered with mustard seeds, and powdered mustard is used in pickles to give a sour taste. Bottled mustard paste is used for salad dressing and accompaniments.

Nutmeg (*jaiphal*): It is oval with a spicy flavor and aroma and is always used grated. It is used to flavor vegetables, soups, cakes, and puddings.

Saffron (*kesar*): Saffron strands are dried stigmas of the saffron crocus flower. It is an expensive and exotic spice. Saffron strands are generally infused in hot water or hot milk to extract its color and delicate flavor.

Sesame (*til*) **seeds**: These are generally found in two colors: white and brown. It has a nutty taste and emits more flavor when roasted. Roasted seeds are ground and mixed to prepare desserts and savory dishes.

Turmeric (*haldi*) **powder**: It is a root which resembles fresh ginger. It is bright yellow in color. Powdered turmeric is an important ingredient in Indian curries and has an earthy, bitter flavor. It also acts as an antibacterial agent.

KNOW YOUR VEGETABLES

LEAFY GREENS

Spinach (*palak*): Spinach has dark green, smooth leaves and is generally cooked, but the young leaves are often used in salads. It has a bitter-sweet flavor. The most common way to prepare spinach is by sautéing with other vegetables or lentils.

Scallion (*hara pyaz*): Also known as green onion, this vegetable normally has small white bulbs at the tip and is ideal for stir-fry dishes. Scallion has a mild flavor and is, therefore, relished in salads.

Mint (*pudina*): The leaves have a fresh aromatic, sweet flavor with a menthol after taste. Mint leaves are also used in beverages and ice creams.

Fenugreek (*methi*): Fenugreek leaves have a strong, bitter flavor with a characteristic aroma.

Curry leaves (*kadhi patta*): Curry leaves come from the curry tree, a short tree whose leaves resemble those of the neem plant. The leaves are commonly used for seasoning. They can also be used in the dried form, but fresh leaves have a superior aroma.

Cilantro (*dhaniya*): All parts of this leafy plant are edible. Heat diminishes the flavor of cilantro leaves very quickly and hence they are most commonly used in the final step of preparing a dish, typically as a garnish. The leaves are best stored refrigerated, in airtight containers.

Lemon grass: Lemon grass has a strong lemon-like flavor and is the main ingredient in Thai cuisine. The stems of fresh lemon grass are tough. The chopped grass can be bruised to release its flavor, if used whole in cooking then remove before serving.

GREEN VEGETABLES

Zucchini: Zucchini is a variety of squash, with shiny, edible outer skin. The flesh is white inside with a delicate flavor. Yellow zucchini is also available.

Raw mango (*kairi*): It is a large tropical fruit found in many varieties; raw mango is oblong and greenish. It is primarily used for making pickles and chutneys.

Okra (*bhindi*): Also known as lady's finger, okra is fairly popular in Indian cuisine. It looks like a capsule about 2-5 inches long. Its big white seeds are tender when cooked and contribute a lot to the flavor of the vegetable.

Green peas (*hara mattar*): Also known as garden peas, these are bright green pods. The peas inside are glossy, crunchy, and sweet. Shell just before using. Green peas are a fair source of vitamins A and C and iron.

Green chili: The most commonly used vegetable in Indian cooking is the small green chili. A good substitute for this could be the Thai green chili. It has a very sharp and pungent spiciness, and is frequently used to flavor a dish right from the start.

Green banana (*kacha kela*): Green banana is used in many parts of India. It is hard and crunchy when raw. It softens when heated or pressure cooked and has a fibrous texture.

Green beans: These are mostly fat and fleshy, and firm when fresh. Steamed and sautéed, beans can also be used in salads. Green beans contain a fair amount of vitamins A and C.

Broccoli: Broccoli belongs to the cabbage family, and has fleshy, dark green flower heads. It is quick and easy to prepare, and can be eaten boiled or steamed or raw with a dip of your choice. Broccoli is also used in soups and side dishes.

Bell pepper (*Shimla mirch*): Bell pepper and chilies are members of the capsicum family. Green bell pepper has a fresh raw flavor, whereas the red, yellow, and orange ones are sweeter. Pepper can be fried with onion and garlic, braised with tomatoes, combined with potatoes, and used raw in salads.

ROOT VEGETABLES

Potato: Potato is a starchy, tuberous root vegetable. It is an important source of carbohydrates. It also contains potassium, iron, and vitamins B and C. Potato can be boiled, baked, deep-fried, sautéed, mashed, or roasted.

Sweet potato (*shakarkandi*): Sweet potato is a starchy and sweet-tasting root vegetable. The skin color ranges from white to pink to reddish brown. Sweet potato can be baked or boiled and has a distinct sweet and savory flavor. It is used in savory and salad dishes.

Carrot (*gajar*): Carrot is a root vegetable, either orange or red in color, with a crisp texture when fresh. It has a sweet and fragrant flavor when eaten raw. Carrot can be cooked in many ways. Carrot juice is a healthy drink and can also be blended with salad dressing. It is rich in carotene and vitamin A.

Colocasia (*arvi*): Colocasia is a round or elongated tuberous, hairy root vegetable. It is boiled like potato, peeled, and then used. It has a sticky flesh.

Ginger (*adrak*): Fresh ginger is pale in color with knobbly roots. Ginger's flavor is peppery and slightly sweet, while its aroma is pungent and spicy. Ginger enhances and complements both sweet and savory food. It is used to spice cookies, cakes, tea, coffee, jams, and pickles.

Radish (*mooli*): Radish can be found in multiple varieties. The one most commonly used in Indian cooking is in the Daikon family. It has long, white, elongated, and smooth roots. The raw flesh of these roots has a crisp and crunchy texture. The taste is pungent and sharp – almost peppery.

GOURDS

Bitter gourd (*karela*): Also known as bitter melon, this is a fruit with a warty texture on the outside. The flesh part is thin and the entire fruit is almost hollow with large seeds. It is best cooked when it is green and unripened. This vegetable has a strong bitter flavor. Salting, followed by washing, can mitigate the bitterness a little.

Bottle gourd (*lauki*): Also known as calabash, bottle gourd is large and hollow. The freshest samples have a light green skin and white flesh. It is cooked most often like a squash. It can be the main ingredient in a lot of recipes but also complements other dishes like lentils very well.

Ridge gourd (*turai*): Ridge gourd has even ridges running down the exterior at regular intervals. It is typically harvested before maturity. At that stage it is light green in color and has tender flesh.

Cucumber (*khira*): Cucumber is a long, green, cylindrical fruit of the gourd family with edible seeds and crisp flesh. It is normally eaten raw in salads. The young cucumber is used for making pickles.

MISCELLANEOUS VEGETABLES

 Cauliflower (*phool gobi*): While cauliflower is available in many colors, the most popular among these is the white variety. It can be prepared in a number of ways: boiled, roasted, fried, steamed or even eaten raw. It is low in fat and high in dietary fiber and vitamin C.

 Cabbage (*bandh gobi*): Cabbage is widely used in Indian cooking. The part of the plant normally consumed is the immature bunch of leaves that are light green in color. It is most often prepared by sautéing and also complements other vegetables such as peas and potatoes.

 Onion (*pyaz*): Onion is an integral part of Indian cuisine. It adds a delicate aroma when cooked and a sharp taste when used raw as a garnish.

 Pearl onion: Pearl onion is most commonly used in stews. However, it can just easily be used in saucy and dry dishes alike. The flavor is sweeter than normal onions.

 Garlic (*lasan*): Garlic is widely used for its pungent flavor. It is typically paired with ginger for a richer, aromatic taste. It has a very long shelf life and is typically stored in warm dry conditions.

 **Tomato:** The tomato found in India is very similar to the Italian Roma tomato. It is widely used in Indian cooking, especially as a base for sauces. It is also frequently consumed in its raw form.

 **Cherry tomato:** Cherry tomato is the smaller variety of the traditional tomato. It is a little sweeter in taste and is most commonly served raw in salads.

 Lemon (*nimbu*): Freshly squeezed lemon juice adds great flavor to most foods. The acidity it provides can really enrich the taste of an otherwise bland dish.

 Pumpkin (*kaddu, kaashiphal*): The pumpkin found in India is typically dark orange and sometimes almost red. It tends to have a thick flesh but is otherwise mostly hollow and contains a mesh of seeds. The seeds aren't typically used in cooking but the flesh is consumed widely.

 Baby corn (*bhutta*): Baby corn is harvested premature corn, which is typically 2-4 inches long. It is consumed whole on the cob. It is tender and provides a nice crunchiness.

GOODNESS OF LEGUMES

Legumes are the edible seeds of peas and beans. Highly nutritious, legumes can be used in soups, curries, or as an accompanying vegetable. A variety of legumes exist with colors that range from yellow to red-orange to green, brown, and black. They are sold in many forms, with or without the skins, whole or split. They contain high levels of proteins, vitamin B1, dietary fiber, and minerals.

Yellow Lentil
(*arhar dal*)

Dehusked Split Black Lentil
(*dhuli urad dal*)

Whole Red Lentil
(*kale masoor*)

Split Green Lentil
(*dhuli moong dal*)

Red Gram Lentil
(*malka masoor*)

White Peas
(*safed mattar*)

Dehusked Split Bengal Gram
(*chana dal*)

Black-eyed Pea
(*lobhia*)

Chickpeas
(*kabuli chana*)

Black Gram
(*kala chana*)

Split Green Gram
(*chilka moong dal*)

Green Lentil
(*sabut moong dal*)

Kidney Beans
(*rajmah*)

Dry Lentil Dumplings
(*magori*)

KITCHEN EQUIPMENT

Pressure cooker

Skillet

Grater (*kaddu kas*)

Griddle (*tawa*)

Deep-frying wok (*kadhai*)

Deep strainer

Saucepan

Measuring cup

Idlí stand

Colander (*chalni*)

Spice box (*masala dani*)

Tongs (*chimta*)

Strainer (*chai ki chalni*)

Sieve / Sifter (*chhanni*)

Tempering ladle
(*chouk ki kalchi*)

Rolling board and rolling pin
(*chakla-belan*)

Chopping board

Mortar and pestle (*moosal*)

Potato masher

Wire whisk

Vegetable peeler

Melon scoop

Knives (*churi / chaku*)

Pancake turner (*palta*)

Spatula (*jharni*)

Ladle (*kalchi*)

Slotted spoon (*Boondi* ladle)

DRINKS, SOUPS & SALADS

SPICED YOGURT DRINK
Mattha

Serves: 4

INGREDIENTS
1 cup Yogurt (*dahi*)
½ tsp Roasted cumin (*jeera*) powder (see p. 184)
Salt to taste
¼ tsp Mint (*pudina*) powder (see p. 11)
¼ tsp Black salt (*kala namak*)
2 cups Water
Cilantro (*dhaniya*) leaves, chopped for garnishing

METHOD
- Whisk the yogurt. Add roasted cumin powder, salt to taste, mint powder, and black salt. Stir to mix well.

- Add water and mix well.

- Serve chilled garnished with cilantro leaves.

• Spiced yogurt drink gives a cool refreshing feeling during summer.

ICED TEA
Sharbati Chai

INGREDIENTS

For the tea syrup:

1 ¼ cups Sugar
1 cup Water
6 tbsp Lemon grass, chopped
5 tsp Tea leaves
2 tbsp Lemon (*nimbu*) juice

For each serving:

2 tbsp Prepared tea syrup
2 tsp Lemon juice
2 tsp Honey
Ice cubes
2 Lemon, slices
8 Mint (*pudina*) leaves
½ cup Chilled water

METHOD

• **For the tea syrup**, mix sugar, water, and lemon grass in a pan. Boil on low heat until the sugar dissolves. Add tea leaves and turn off the heat. Leave covered and set aside for 20 minutes.

• Strain the tea mixture, cool, and add 2 tbsp lemon juice. Set aside.

• In each serving glass, put 2 tbsp tea syrup, 2 tsp lemon juice, 2 tsp honey, and fill with ice cubes.

• Add lemon slices and mint leaves. Fill with chilled water and serve.

• Iced tea is an unusually flavored substitute for carbonated drinks.

MANGO MOCKTAIL
Aam Panna

INGREDIENTS
2 Raw mangoes (*kairi*), medium-sized, pressure cooked, peeled, pulp removed
(see p. 183)
Salt to taste
4 tbsp Mint (*pudina*) leaves
2 tbsp Confectioners' sugar
1 tsp Roasted cumin (*jeera*) powder (see p. 184)
For each serving:
Gram flour granules (*boondi*, see p. 168), crushed ice and mint sprigs

METHOD
• Blend the mango pulp with 4 cups water, salt to taste, and mint leaves.

• Strain the mixture in a sieve.

• Add sugar and roasted cumin powder to the mango mixture; mix well and chill.

• Put crushed ice in each glass, pour the drink, and serve garnished with 2 tsp gram flour granules and mint sprigs.

• Two mangoes will give approximately 1½ cups of pulp.
• Mango mocktail is a good summer drink as it prevents heat stroke.

• Gram flour granule (*boondi*) packets are available in any Indian grocery store.

ORANGE GLORY
Narangi Savera

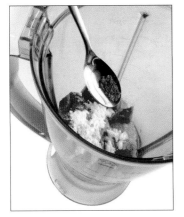

INGREDIENTS

3-4 Oranges (*santara*), peeled, broken into segments, chilled
5 oz Papaya (*papita*), cut into medium-sized cubes, chilled
2 tbsp Confectioners' Sugar
¼ tsp Black salt (*kala namak*)
1½ cups Water
1 tsp Lemon (*nimbu*) juice
Crushed ice for serving

METHOD

• Blend the chilled oranges and cut papaya with sugar, black salt, and water in a mixer.

• Strain and add lemon juice.

• Put crushed ice into individual glasses, pour the fruit mixture, and serve.

• Red papaya tastes better in this drink.

• This is a delightful and healthy breakfast drink.

TENDER COCONUT COOLER
Daab Shikanji

Serves: 4

INGREDIENTS

2 cups Tender coconut water (*daab*), chilled
2 cups Lemon soda, chilled
½ tsp Black salt (*kala namak*)
2 tsp Honey

For the garnishing:
1 tbsp Tender coconut flesh (*malai*), chopped
1 tsp Cilantro (*dhaniya*) leaves, chopped
¼ lb Papaya (*papita*)

METHOD

- Scoop out 8 papaya balls with a fruit scooper and keep aside.

- Mix coconut water, lemon soda, black salt, and honey together.

- Pour into individual glasses. Serve garnished with chopped tender coconut flesh, cilantro leaves, and papaya balls.

- Tender coconut water is rich in mineral salts.
- It acts as a coolant for the digestive system.

- The flesh of the tender coconut has a soft creamy texture and can be easily scooped out and chopped.

MINTY LEMONADE
Hara Bhara Nimbu Pani

INGREDIENTS
1 tbsp Lemon (*nimbu*) juice
1½ tbsp Sugar
¼ tsp Black salt (*kala namak*)
4-6 Mint (*pudina*) leaves
¾ cup Water
Ice for serving

METHOD
- Put lemon juice, sugar, black salt, mint, and water into a jar and mix well.
- Pour into a tall serving glass.
- Serve with ice.

- Minty lemonade is a healthy substitute for carbonated drinks.
- Calorie watchers can use sugar substitutes.

TOMATO CUCUMBER MELODY
Tamatar Khira Lajawab

INGREDIENTS

4 Tomatoes, medium-sized, cut into 8 pieces
2 cups Water
Salt to taste
¼ tsp Black pepper (*kali mirch*)
2 tsp Confectioners' Sugar

For serving: mix together
2 tbsp Cucumber (*khira*), finely chopped
1 tbsp Bell pepper (*Shimla mirch*), finely chopped
½ tbsp Mint (*pudina*), chopped
½ tbsp Cilantro (*dhaniya*) leaves, chopped

METHOD

• Heat 5 cups water for 4 minutes; turn off the heat. Add the tomatoes and leave them covered for half an hour. Remove and chill the tomatoes.

• Blend the chilled tomatoes with 2 cups water and strain.

• Add salt, black pepper, and sugar. Mix and chill.

• **For serving**, put 1 tbsp chopped vegetable mixture into individual glasses, fill with tomato juice and serve.

• Do not liquify the tomatoes without blanching, to ensure that the pulp and liquid do not separate.

• Tomato Cucumber Melody makes a healthy, refreshing lunchtime drink.

CARROT SOUP
Gajar Shorba

INGREDIENTS

4 Carrots (*gajar*), medium-sized, cut into cubes
1 Potato, medium-sized, cut into cubes
2 tsp Butter
2 tsp Cilantro (*dhaniya*) leaf paste
Salt to taste
6 Black peppercorns (*sabut kali mirch*), crushed
½ tsp Sugar

METHOD

- Heat 1 tsp butter in a pressure cooker for 30 seconds; add carrots and potato and cook for a minute. Add 3½ cups water and pressure cook until one whistle. Cool, blend and strain. Set aside.

- Grind the cilantro leaves in a mortar to a fine paste.

- Heat 1 tsp butter in a pan; add cilantro leaf paste and sauté for 10 seconds. Add the strained vegetable mixture, salt, black pepper, and sugar; bring to the boil, and simmer for 2 minutes. Serve hot.

- Carrot soup is a quick healthy soup which can be prepared with red or orange carrots.

- This soup can be garnished with cream or freshly ground pepper, if desired.

GREEN PEA SOUP
Mattar Shorba

Serves: 4-6

INGREDIENTS

For the soup stock:

2 cups Green peas (*hara mattar*), shelled

2 cups Spinach (*palak*), chopped

1 tbsp Mint (*pudina*), chopped

Other Ingredients

2 tsp Butter

1 cup Milk

Salt and black pepper (*kali mirch*) to taste

¼ tsp Sugar

¼ tsp Ground nutmeg (*jaiphal*)

2 tsp Lemon (*nimbu*) juice

Fried bread croutons for garnishing

METHOD

• **For the soup stock**, melt 1 tsp butter in a pressure cooker, add green peas, spinach, and mint; cook for 30 seconds. Add 2½ cups water and pressure cook until one whistle. Simmer for 2 minutes.

• Remove, cool, blend and strain.

• Melt 1 tsp butter in a pan; add strained soup stock, milk, salt, black pepper to taste, sugar, and ground nutmeg. Bring to a boil, simmer for 2 minutes and then remove from heat.

• Add lemon juice and croutons just before serving.

• Mint adds a unique flavor to the soup.
• To retain the green color of the soup, remove the lid from the pressure cooker after the pressure drops and cover the soup with a wire mesh.

SPINACH SOUP
Palak Shorba

Serves: 4

INGREDIENTS

8 cups Spinach (*palak*),
chopped, washed
½ tsp Sugar
1 tsp Butter
1 cup Milk
Salt and black pepper (*kali mirch*) to taste
¼ tsp Ground nutmeg (*jaiphal*)
Cream for garnishing

METHOD

- Boil 5 cups water, add spinach and ¼ tsp sugar; cook for 4 minutes and drain. Cool and blend with 2½ cups water.

- Melt 1 tsp butter in a pan; add blended spinach, milk, salt, black pepper to taste, nutmeg, and ¼ tsp sugar.

- Bring the mixture to a boil, simmer for 2 minutes and remove from heat.

- Serve hot garnished with cream.

- Spinach soup is enriched with iron and is very good for growing children.

- The calorie conscious can omit the cream.

TOMATO SOUP
Tamatar Shorba

INGREDIENTS

6 Tomatoes, medium-sized, ripe, cut into 8 pieces
2 Carrots (*gajar*), medium-sized, cut into cubes
1 tsp Butter
Salt to taste
½ tsp Sugar
1 tsp Roasted cumin (*jeera*) powder (see p. 184)
¼ tsp Black peppercorns (*sabut kali mirch*), freshly ground

For the garnishing:
1 cup Fried bread croutons
Cilantro (*dhaniya*) leaves, chopped
Heavy cream

METHOD

• Pressure cook the tomatoes and carrots with 2 cups water until one whistle.

• Set aside to cool. Blend and strain.

• Melt 1 tsp butter in a pan; add strained tomato mixture, salt to taste, sugar, roasted cumin powder, and ground black pepper. Bring to a boil and simmer for 5 minutes.

• Serve hot garnished with fried bread croutons, cilantro leaves, and heavy cream.

• Tomato soup is a popular and all-time favorite soup.
• Carrots give this soup its body and additional flavor.

• Bread croutons are ½" cubes, deep-fried or sautéed until crisp.

VEGETABLE GARDEN SOUP
Sabz Baghan Shorba

Serves: 4-6

INGREDIENTS

2 tbsp Green gram (*dhuli moong dal*), washed, soaked for 30 minutes

2 Tomatoes, large, cut into 8 pieces

1 Carrot (*gajar*), medium-sized, cut into cubes

1 tsp Butter

½ cup Carrots, grated

½ cup White cabbage (*bandh gobi*), shredded

½ cup Tomatoes, chopped

Salt and black pepper (*kali mirch*) to taste

¼ tsp Sugar

2 tsp Lemon (*nimbu*) juice

½ cup Spinach (*palak*), finely chopped

METHOD

• Pressure cook the soaked green gram, tomatoes, and carrot with 3 cups water until one whistle. Cool, blend and strain.

• Melt 1 tsp butter in a pan; add grated carrots, shredded cabbage, and chopped tomatoes; sauté for 30 seconds. Add the strained tomato mixture, salt, black pepper to taste, and sugar.

• Bring the mixture to a boil and simmer for 5 minutes. Remove from heat.

• Add lemon juice and chopped spinach, mix and serve hot.

• This soup can be garnished with fried bread croutons.

• This is a healthy soup with a combination of lentil and vegetables.

CHICKPEA SOUP
Kabuli Chana Shorba

Serves: 4-6

INGREDIENTS
1 cup Chickpeas (*kabuli chana*), boiled (see p. 193)
1 cup Potatoes, chopped
2 tsp Butter
¼ cup Onion, chopped
½ tsp Ground cumin (*jeera*)
½ tsp Garlic (*lasan*), chopped
½ tsp Ginger (*adrak*) paste (see p.191)
1 cup Spinach (*palak*), finely chopped
Salt to taste
Black peppercorns (*sabut kali mirch*) freshly ground to taste
Lemon (*nimbu*) juice to taste

METHOD
- Melt 1 tsp butter in a pressure cooker; add onion and cook for a minute. Add the potatoes and cook for 30 seconds. Add 3 cups water and pressure cook until one whistle, cool, blend, and strain.

- Melt 1 tsp butter in a pan; add cumin, garlic, ginger paste, and spinach. Cook for 30 seconds.

- Add boiled chickpeas, strained onion-potato mixture, salt and black pepper to taste; bring to a boil, and simmer for 2 minutes.

- Add lemon juice to taste and serve hot.

- This is a wholesome soup with a good combination of proteins and carbohydrates.

- All soups taste best when served fresh.

CHICKPEA SALAD
Kabuli Chana Salaad

Serves: 4-6

INGREDIENTS

¾ cup Chickpeas (*kabuli chana*),
boiled, strained
(see p. 193)

For the dressing:
1½ tbsp Lemon (*nimbu*) juice
2 tsp Confectioners' Sugar
1 tbsp Cilantro (*dhaniya*) leaves,
chopped
½ tsp Salt
¼ tsp Red chili flakes

For the tempering:
1 tbsp Vegetable oil
¼ tsp Mustard seeds
12 Curry leaves (*kadhi patta*)

For the garnishing:
2 tbsp Coconut (*nariyal*), grated
1 tbsp Cilantro leaves, chopped

METHOD

- **For the dressing**, combine all the ingredients together.

- Mix the dressing with the boiled chickpeas. Cover with plastic wrap and chill for an hour.

- **For the tempering**, heat 1 tbsp oil in a pan for 30 seconds; add mustard seeds and curry leaves. Pour over chilled salad, just before serving.

- Serve garnished with grated coconut and cilantro leaves.

- This unusual salad, with the delicate flavor of coconut, is tempered with South Indian spices.

CORN SALAD
Makai Salaad

INGREDIENTS
1¾ cup Sweet corn (*makai*)
½ cup Yellow bell pepper,
chopped into medium-sized cubes
½ cup Red bell pepper, chopped
into medium-sized cubes
¼ cup Scallions (*hara pyaz*),
chopped
2 tsp Vegetable oil
½ cup Fried noodles for
garnishing

For the dressing:
1½ tbsp Vegetable oil
1 tbsp White / Balsamic vinegar
(*sirka*)
¼ tsp Salt
¼ tsp Black peppercorns (*sabut
kali mirch*), freshly ground
1 tsp Confectioners' sugar

METHOD
- Heat 2 tsp oil in a pan; add the corn and cook for a minute. Set aside to cool (see p. 197). Refrigerate corn and chopped vegetables until further use.

- **For the dressing**, mix all the ingredients together and set aside.

- Mix the corn and vegetables with the dressing just before serving.

- Serve chilled, garnished with fried noodles.

- Cut vegetables for salad should always be covered with plastic wrap before chilling.
- Olive oil and refined peanut oil can also be used for the dressing.
- Noodles are always deep-fried after boiling.

CUCUMBER SALAD WITH YOGURT DRESSING
Dahi Kakdi

INGREDIENTS

2 Cucumber (*khira*), medium-sized

1 tbsp Peanuts (*moongphalli*), coarsely powdered (see p.185)

For the dressing:

½ cup Yogurt (*dahi*), thick (see p. 198)

2 tsp White / Balsamic vinegar (*sirka*)

2 tsp Confectioners' sugar,

¼ tsp Salt

1 tsp Mint (*pudina*), chopped

METHOD

• Cut cucumber into slices and chill.

• **For the dressing**, mix all the ingredients together and refrigerate.

• Layer the dressing over the cucumber slices just before serving.

• Serve chilled garnished with peanuts.

• Drain 1½ cups yogurt in a strainer for 30 minutes to make ½ cup thick yogurt.

• Use baby cucumber or English cucumber for better taste.

POTATO AND PICKLED ONION SALAD
Aloo Pyaz, Sirkewale

INGREDIENTS
6 Potatoes, medium-sized
1¼ cups Pickled onions (see p. 164)
½ cup Scallions (*hara pyaz*), chopped
1½ tbsp Vegetable oil

For the dressing: mix and set aside
¾ tsp Salt
½ tsp Black peppercorns (*sabut kali mirch*), freshly ground
2 tsp Confectioners' sugar
2 tsp Mint (*pudina*) leaves, coarsely pounded
½ tsp Mustard (*sarson*) powder
1 tbsp White / Balsamic vinegar (*sirka*)
½ tsp Ginger (*adrak*) paste
2 tsp Lemon (*nimbu*) juice

For the garnishing:
1 tbsp Cilantro (*dhaniya*) leaves, chopped
2 tbsp Peanuts (*moongphalli*), skinned

METHOD
- Apply ½ tbsp oil to the potatoes. Bake at 400° F for 25-35 minutes or until soft (see p. 182). Peel and cut the potatoes into 1" cubes.

- Heat 1 tbsp oil in a pan; add the potatoes and sauté on medium heat until light golden brown. Remove and set aside to cool.

- Mix the sautéed potatoes, pickled onions, and scallions with the dressing just before serving.

- Serve garnished with cilantro leaves and peanuts.

- Baked and sautéed potatoes seasoned with *chaat masala* can be served as a tasty snack with drinks.

SALAD MEDLEY WITH JAGGERY DRESSING
Mila Jula Salaad

INGREDIENTS

2 Cucumbers (*khira*), medium-sized, cut into medium-sized cubes
1 Carrot (*gajar*), cut into medium-sized cubes
1 Tomato, cut into medium-sized cubes
1 Apple (*seb*), cut into medium-sized cubes
¼ cup Sweet corn (*makai*)

For the dressing:
1 tbsp Vegetable oil
¼ tsp Red chili flakes
2 tsp Jaggery (*gur*)
2 tsp Lemon (*nimbu*) juice
¼ tsp Mint (*pudina*) powder (see p. 11)
¼ tsp Salt

METHOD

- Cut the vegetables, cover with plastic wrap, and chill in the refrigerator.

- **For the dressing**, heat 1 tbsp oil in a pan for 30 seconds. Add red chili flakes and cook for 10 seconds. Add jaggery and mix well.

- Turn off the heat, and cool the mixture. Add lemon juice, mint powder, and salt; keep aside.

- Mix the dressing with the chilled vegetables and cut apple just before serving.

- Jaggery is made by boiling raw sugarcane juice and is used extensively in Indian cooking. It gives a unique flavor to the salad.

- Sprinkle 1 tsp lemon juice on cut apple to prevent browning.

SWEET POTATO AND BEAN SPROUT SALAD
Chatpata Shakarkandi Salaad

INGREDIENTS

1 lb Sweet potatoes (*shakarkandi*)
1 oz Bean sprouts
4 oz Iceberg lettuce
1-2 tbsp Vegetable oil for shallow-frying

For the dressing: mix and set aside

1½ tbsp Lemon (*nimbu*) juice
3 tsp *Chaat masala*
2 tbsp Cilantro (*dhaniya*) leaves, chopped
½ tsp Salt

METHOD

- Apply oil to the sweet potatoes. Bake at 400°F for 20-30 minutes until soft (see p. 182). Peel and cut into ¼" discs.

- Heat 2 tbsp oil in a pan for 60 seconds and shallow-fry the discs on medium heat until light golden brown.

- Remove from the heat and place onto a plate.

- Add dressing just before serving.

- Arrange the discs on a serving plate and garnish with bean sprouts and lettuce.

- Applying oil to the sweet potatoes helps to peel the skin easily.
- Instead of baking, sweet potatoes can also be pressure cooked.

- Sweet potato discs with dressing can also be served as an appetizer.

TOMATO AND COTTAGE CHEESE SALAD
Tamatar aur Masala Paneer Salaad

INGREDIENTS

4 Tomatoes, firm, medium-sized, quartered, pulp removed (see p.186)

5 oz Masala cottage cheese (*paneer*) (see p.188), cut into small cubes, chilled

4 Lettuce leaves, large

For the seasoning:

1 tbsp Olive / Vegetable oil

2 tsp White / Balsamic vinegar (*sirka*)

2 tsp Confectioners' Sugar

¼ tsp Mustard (*sarson*) powder

¼ tsp Mint (*pudina*) powder (see p. 11)

¼ tsp Black peppercorns (*sabut kali mirch*), freshly ground

¼ tsp Salt

METHOD

- **For the seasoning**, mix all the ingredients together.

- Apply ¾ of the seasoning to the tomato skins.

- Mix the remaining ¼ of the seasoning with the cubed masala cottage cheese.

- Arrange the seasoned tomato skins on a serving plate. Put 1 tbsp cottage cheese mixture on each tomato skin.

- Serve chilled garnished with a fan formation of lettuce leaves.

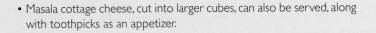

- Masala cottage cheese, cut into larger cubes, can also be served, along with toothpicks as an appetizer.

SNACKS & APPETIZERS

CORN ON TOAST
Karare Makai Pav

INGREDIENTS

4 Bread slices
¾ cup Sweet corn (*makai*)
1 tbsp Celery, chopped
¼ cup White sauce (see below)
Vegetable oil for deep-frying
Cilantro (*dhaniya*) leaves
and Tomatoes, chopped for
garnishing

For the white sauce:

2 tsp Vegetable oil
1 tsp All-purpose flour (*maida*)
½ cup Milk
Salt and black pepper (*kali mirch*) to taste
¼ tsp Sugar
2 tsp Processed cheese, grated

METHOD

- **For the white sauce**, heat 2 tsp oil in a pan for 30 seconds; add flour and sauté for 10 seconds, turn off the heat. Add milk and the remaining ingredients for white sauce and mix well. Turn on the heat again and bring mixture to a boil, stirring constantly. Remove and set aside.

- Mix the corn and celery in the white sauce and set aside.

- Cut each slice of bread into 4 triangles and remove the crusts.

- Heat 1"-deep oil in a shallow pan; deep-fry the bread triangles in hot oil until light golden brown. Remove with

a slotted spoon.

- Put 1 tsp of corn mixture on each piece of bread, garnish with tomatoes and cilantro leaves and serve hot.

- Use day-old bread, as it absorbs less oil.
- Use milk that is room temperature and be sure to turn off the heat, as instructed in the white sauce preparation, to avoid lumps.

- Calorie watchers can toast the bread instead of frying.
- This snack makes a good appetizer with drinks.
- Serve with tomato sauce and red chili sauce.

CRISPY BABY CORN
Chhote Karare Bhutte

INGREDIENTS

12 Baby corn (*bhutta*)
Vegetable oil for deep-frying

For the batter:
2 tbsp All-purpose flour (*maida*)
2 tbsp Cornstarch
2 tsp White sesame (*til*) seeds
1 tbsp Celery, chopped
¼ tsp Baking powder
¼ tsp Black pepper (*kali mirch*)
¼ tsp Salt
¼ tsp Sugar
Water to make semi-thick batter

METHOD

• **For the batter**, mix all the ingredients mentioned and prepare a semi-thick batter with water.

• Coat each baby corn with the prepared batter.

• Heat 1"-deep oil in a shallow pan; deep-fry baby corn in medium-hot oil, until light golden brown.

• Remove with a slotted spoon and serve hot.

• If the baby corn are thick, slit them into two, vertically.
• This snack makes a good appetizer for parties.

• This snack can be half-fried ahead of time and re-fried for a minute in hot oil, just before serving.

COTTAGE CHEESE FRITTERS
Paneer Pakodi

INGREDIENTS

1 lb Cottage cheese (*paneer*)
(see p. 188), cut into 2" X 2"
block, ½" thick
Vegetable oil for deep-frying
Chaat masala to sprinkle

For the filling: mix together
3 tsp Ginger (*adrak*) paste (see
p. 191)
1½ tsp Green chili paste (see
p. 191)
2 tsp Cilantro (*dhaniya*) paste
½ tsp *Chaat masala*
¼ tsp Salt
1 tsp Lemon (*nimbu*) juice mix

For the batter:
1½ cups Gram flour (*besan*)
¼ tsp Baking powder
¼ tsp Carom (*ajwain*) seeds
½ tsp Salt
½ cup Water (approx.) to
make semi-thick batter

METHOD

• Slit ½" -thick blocks of
cottage cheese horizontally
into 2 slices. Put ½ tsp layer
of filling on one slice and
cover with the second slice.

• **For the batter**, mix all the
ingredients together and
prepare a semi-thick batter
with water.

• Press the filled 2 slices of
cottage cheese together and
coat with the batter on all
sides. Heat 1"-deep oil in a
shallow pan; deep-fry cottage
cheese in medium-hot oil
until light golden brown.

• Remove with a slotted
spoon.

• Cut each into 2 pieces,
place the cut side up on the
serving plate, sprinkle *chaat
masala* and serve hot.

• Use fresh cottage cheese.
• Serve as an appetizer to a meal or as an afternoon snack.

FLORET FRITTERS
Gobi Pakodi

INGREDIENTS

1 Cauliflower (*phool gobi*), medium-sized, cut into 20 florets
Vegetable oil for deep-frying
Chaat masala and Cilantro (*dhaniya*) leaves, chopped for garnishing

For the batter:

1½ cups Gram flour (*besan*)
¼ tsp Baking powder
¾ tsp Carom (*ajwain*) seeds
$\frac{1}{8}$ tsp Asafetida (*hing*)
¾ tsp Salt
2 tsp Ginger (*adrak*) paste (see p. 191)
1 tsp Green chili paste (see p. 191)
2 tbsp Cilantro leaves, chopped
1 tbsp Coriander (*dhaniya*) seeds, crushed
¾ cup Water (approx.) to make semi-thick batter

METHOD

- Boil 5 cups water, add ½ tsp salt and cauliflower florets and cook for a minute. Remove and drain.

- **For the batter**, mix all the ingredients together and prepare a semi-thick batter with water.

- Coat the cooked cauliflower florets with the batter. Heat 1"-deep oil in a shallow pan; deep-fry the florets in medium-hot oil for 30 seconds; remove and cool.

- Press it slightly, re-fry in hot oil until light golden brown.

- Sprinkle *chaat masala* and cilantro leaves. Serve hot.

- Be careful not to over-boil the cauliflower as this will increase its oil absorption.
- Floret fritters are an excellent accompaniment to any meal and can also be served as a snack.
- Serve with green chutney (see p. 154) / sweet chutney (see p. 157) and tomato sauce.

POTATO FRITTERS
Aloo Pakodi

INGREDIENTS

2 Potatoes, medium-sized, cut into discs, immersed in water
Vegetable oil for deep-frying
Chaat masala and Cilantro (*dhaniya*) leaves, chopped for garnishing

For the batter:

1½ cups Gram flour (*besan*)
½ tsp Carom (*ajwain*) seeds
a pinch Asafetida (*hing*)
1 tsp Ginger (*adrak*) paste (see p. 191)
½ tsp Green chili paste (see p. 191)
½ tsp Red chili powder
½ tsp Salt
¼ tsp Baking powder
¾ cup Fenugreek (*methi*) leaves, chopped
½ cup Water (approx.) to make semi-thick batter

METHOD

• **For the batter**, mix all the ingredients together and prepare a semi-thick batter.

• Coat the potato slices with batter on both sides.

• Heat 1"-deep oil in a shallow pan; deep-fry the potato slices in medium-hot oil until light golden brown. Remove with a slotted spoon.

• Sprinkle *chaat masala* and cilantro leaves, and serve hot.

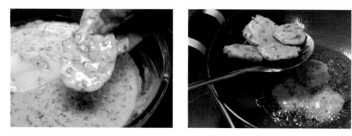

• Serve with green chutney (see p. 154), sweet chutney (see p. 157) or tomato sauce.

• This is a perfect snack to eat with hot tea on a rainy afternoon.

• Potato fritters are quick to prepare when unexpected guests drop in.

STUFFED CHILI FRITTERS
Bharwa Mirchi ki Pakodi

Serves: 4-6

INGREDIENTS

12 Light green chilies, large
Vegetable oil for deep-frying
Chaat masala and Cilantro
(*dhaniya*) leaves, chopped for
garnishing

For the stuffing:

2 tsp Vegetable oil
1½ cups Sweet corn (*makai*)
Salt to taste
½ tsp *Chaat masala*
2 tbsp Cilantro leaves, chopped
½ tsp Mint (*pudina*) powder
(see p. 11)
1 tsp Lemon (*nimbu*) juice

For the batter:

1½ cups Gram flour (*besan*)
¼ tsp Baking powder
¼ tsp Carom (*ajwain*) seeds
a pinch Asafetida (*hing*)
½ tsp Salt
¾ cup Water to make a semi-
thick batter

METHOD

- **For the stuffing**, heat 2 tsp oil in a pan; add sweet corn, salt to taste, *chaat masala*, cilantro leaves, and mint powder; cook for a minute. Add lemon juice and mix well. Set aside.

- Slit each green chili vertically with a sharp knife, keeping its shape intact. Fill with the corn stuffing.

- **For the batter**, mix all the ingredients together and prepare a semi-thick batter with water. Coat each chili evenly with batter.

- Heat 1"-deep oil in a shallow pan; deep-fry the green chilies in medium-hot oil until light golden brown. Remove with a slotted spoon.

- Sprinkle *chaat masala* and cilantro leaves and serve hot.

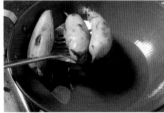

- They can be semi-fried ahead of time, refrigerated and re-fried in hot oil before serving.

- Chilies can be filled with any stuffing of your choice.

SPICY SPINACH FRITTERS
Palak Chaat

INGREDIENTS

20 Spinach (*palak*), leaves
Vegetable oil for deep-frying

For the batter:

1 cup Gram flour (*besan*)
1½ tbsp Rice flour
½ tsp Carom (*ajwain*) seeds
1 tsp Red chili powder
a pinch Asafetida (*hing*)
¼ tsp Baking powder
½ tsp Salt
½ cup Water (approx.) to make semi-thick batter

For serving:

1 cup Potatoes, boiled, chopped (see p. 183)
½ cup Green chutney (see p. 154)
¾ cup Sweet chutney (see p. 157)
1¼ cups Yogurt (*dahi*), beaten
Salt to taste
Red chili powder to taste
Roasted cumin (*jeera*) powder to taste (see p. 184)
Thin *sev* and Cilantro (*dhaniya*) leaves, chopped for garnishing

METHOD

- **For the batter**, mix all the ingredients together and prepare a semi-thick batter with water.

- Coat each spinach leaf with batter, on both sides.

- Heat 1"-deep oil in a shallow pan; deep-fry the spinach leaves in medium-hot oil to light golden brown. Set aside.

- **For serving**, place 2 spinach fritters on each serving plate. Add 2 tsp chopped potatoes, 1 tsp green chutney, 2 tsp sweet chutney, and 1 tbsp yogurt on each spinach fritter. Sprinkle salt, red chili powder, and roasted cumin powder to taste. Garnish with thin *sev* and cilantro leaves. Serve immediately.

- Spices can be adjusted as per taste.
- This can also be served as a side dish at meal times.

- All *chaats* should be arranged just before serving, otherwise they tend to get soggy.

CRISPY LENTIL FINGERS
Mast Dal Paare

INGREDIENTS

¾ cup Split green lentil (*dhuli moong dal*), washed, soaked for 2 hours
2 tsp Ginger (*adrak*), chopped
2 tsp Green chilies, chopped
1½ cups Water for grinding
2 tbsp Vegetable oil
1½ tsp Cumin (*jeera*) seeds
½ tsp Salt
2 tbsp Cilantro (*dhaniya*) leaves, chopped
Vegetable oil for deep-frying

METHOD

- Drain the split green lentil and grind to a smooth paste with ginger, green chilies, and water.

- Heat 2 tbsp oil in a non-stick pan for a minute; add cumin seeds and turn off the heat when the seeds turn brown. Add the lentil paste, salt, and cilantro leaves; mix well.

- Turn on the heat and cook the mixture, stirring constantly, until it leaves the sides of the pan.

- Pour the mixture, evenly, into a greased 8" square dish and cool it completely (3 hours). Cut into rectangular fingers 1½" x ½".

- Heat 1"-deep oil in a shallow pan; deep-fry the fingers in medium-hot oil until light golden brown. Serve hot.

- Turning off the heat after adding lentil paste is important otherwise the lentil mixture will become lumpy.
- Serve this snack at a party with a dip of your choice.

- The lentil mixture can be set ahead of time, refrigerated and fried when required.

DRY GREEN LENTIL
Sookhi Moong Dal

INGREDIENTS

¾ cup Green gram (*dhuli moong dal*), soaked for 2 hours, drained
1 tbsp Vegetable oil
a pinch Asafetida (*hing*)
1 tsp Cumin (*jeera*) seeds
1½ tsp Ginger (*adrak*) paste (see p. 191)
1 tsp Green chili paste (see p. 191)
$\frac{1}{8}$ tsp Turmeric (*haldi*) powder
¾ cup Water (approx.)
Salt to taste

For the garnishing:
½ cup Tomatoes, chopped
2 tbsp Cilantro (*dhaniya*) leaves, chopped

METHOD

• Heat 1 tbsp oil in a pan for 30 seconds; add asafetida, cumin seeds, ginger and green chili pastes, and turmeric powder; cook for 10 seconds.

• Add soaked lentil, ¾ cup water, and salt.

• Cook, covered, on low heat for 10-15 minutes or until done.

• Serve hot, garnished with tomatoes and cilantro leaves.

• Be sure to reduce the heat while cooking since lentils loose water very rapidly.
• This can be served for all meals including breakfast.

• Serve with green chutney (see p. 154) and sweet chutney (see p. 157).

LENTIL PANCAKES
Moong Dal Cheela

INGREDIENTS

1¼ cups Green Gram (*dhuli moong dal*), dehusked, split, soaked for 2 hours, drained
2 tbsp Bengal gram (*chana dal*), dehusked, split, soaked for 2 hours, drained
2 tsp Green chilies, chopped
2 tsp Ginger (*adrak*), chopped
Salt to taste
a pinch Asafetida (*hing*)
2 tbsp Cilantro (*dhaniya*) leaves, chopped
Vegetable oil for frying

For the filling:

1 cup Cottage cheese (*paneer*), chopped (see p. 188)
2 tbsp Cilantro leaves, chopped
Salt to taste

METHOD

• Grind both the soaked lentils, green chilies, and ginger with just enough water to form a smooth batter. Mix the batter with salt, asafetida, and cilantro leaves in a bowl. Keep aside.

• **For the filling,** mix all the ingredients together and set aside.

• Heat a non-stick pan and brush with oil; add 1½ tbsp batter and spread until 6" wide. Add 2 tsp oil around the sides of the pancake and cook until light golden brown. Flip and leave for 30 seconds. Flip again.

• Place 1 tbsp cottage cheese filling, fold and serve hot.

• This is a good breakfast dish, high in protein and carbohydrates.
• It is served as an accompaniment at *chaat* parties.

• Calorie watchers can make oil-free pancakes.

SAVORY LENTIL CAKES
Chatpata Dhokla

INGREDIENTS
1½ cups Gram flour (*besan*)
1 tsp Sugar
1 tsp Salt
1 tsp Citric acid
1 tbsp Vegetable oil
1 cup Water (approx.) to prepare the batter
1 tsp Baking soda

For the tempering:
1 tbsp Vegetable oil
1 tsp Mustard seeds (*rai*)
5 Green chilies, slit
2 tbsp Cilantro (*dhaniya*) leaves, chopped
¼ tsp Turmeric (*haldi*) powder
½ cup Water

For the garnishing:
2 tbsp Coconut (*nariyal*), grated
2 tbsp Cilantro leaves, chopped

METHOD
• Place a greased 8" round steel container (empty) in a double boiler. While the container is being heated, mix gram flour, sugar, salt, citric acid, oil and prepare a batter with water. Add baking soda and keep stirring until it rises to double the quantity. Remove the container from the double boiler and put the batter into the container.

• Place the container back into the double boiler and cook, covered, on high heat for 10 minutes or until done (test with a toothpick). Remove the container from the double boiler and cool the mixture in the container. Cut into large cubes and temper (see below) within the container.

• **For the tempering**, heat 1 tbsp oil in a pan for 30 seconds; add mustard seeds, green chilies, cilantro leaves, turmeric powder, and water. Bring to a boil, remove and pour over the prepared cubes.

• Garnish with coconut and cilantro leaves and serve after a minimum of 15 minutes.

• To ensure lightness, add baking soda just before cooking.
• Insert a toothpick in the center of the pan; if the mixture sticks to the toothpick, cover and cook on low heat for 5 more minutes.

• *Dhokla* can be served for breakfast or at tea time and is a favorite of calorie watchers.
• Smear 2 tsp oil on a round steel container for greasing.

MUSHROOM CROQUETTES
Khumb ke Cutlet

Serves: 4-6

INGREDIENTS
1 Potato, large, boiled, grated
2 Bread slices
1½ tbsp Processed cheese, grated
¼ tsp Salt
Vegetable oil for deep-frying

For the filling:
2 tsp Vegetable oil
2 tbsp Mushrooms (*khumb*), chopped
1 tbsp Bll pepper (*Shimla mirch*), chopped
Salt and black pepper (*kali mirch*) to taste

METHOD
- Dip the bread slices in water and squeeze (see p. 199). Mix bread, potato, cheese, and salt together. Set aside

- **For the filling**, heat 2 tsp oil in the pan; add mushrooms, bell pepper, salt and black pepper to taste. Cook for 30 seconds and remove.

- Divide the potato dough into 15 equal-sized balls. Stuff each ball with ¼ tsp filling, fold to seal the filling inside and reshape.

- Heat 1"-deep oil in a shallow pan; deep-fry the croquettes in medium-hot oil until light golden brown. Serve hot.

- The proportion of bread and potato has to be right otherwise the croquette will break while frying.

- Refrigerate after filling to avoid cheese from fermenting.
- Deep-fry 3-4 croquettes at a time.

MUSHROOM CHEESE TOAST
Khumbi Toast

INGREDIENTS

1 French loaf, cut into 10 thin slanted slices
4 Button mushrooms (*khumb*), cut into thin vertical slices
1 Onion, medium-sized, chopped
2 tsp Soft butter
½ cup Cheddar cheese, grated
Salt and black pepper (*kali mirch*) to taste
1 Bell pepper (*Shimla mirch*), medium-sized, chopped
Red chili flakes to sprinkle

METHOD

- Apply soft butter on each slice of French loaf and place mushroom and onion slices along the length.

- Sprinkle cheese, salt and black pepper to taste. Garnish with bell pepper and red chili flakes.

- Bake at 350°F for 5-8 minutes or until brown.

- Always pre-heat the oven for 15 minutes before baking.
- This makes a good appetizer to serve with drinks.

- Mushroom cheese toast is a favorite among kids.

TOASTED GARDEN SANDWICHES
Hara Bhara Toast

INGREDIENTS
12 Bread slices

For the filling:
6 Beans, cut into 1" pieces
1 Carrot (*gajar*), medium-sized,
cut into 1" pieces
1 cup Cabbage (*bandh gobi*), cut
into 1" pieces
6 Baby corn (*bhutta*), cut into
1" pieces
1 Bell pepper (*Shimla mirch*),
medium-sized, cut into 1" pieces
2 tsp Butter
Salt and black pepper (*kali
mirch*) to taste
2 tsp All-purpose flour (*maida*)
¼ cup Milk
Soft butter for applying on both
sides of the bread

METHOD

• **For the filling**, heat 2 tsp butter in a pan for 30 seconds; add all
the cut vegetables, salt and black pepper. Cover and cook for a
minute.

• Add flour to the vegetables and cook for 30 seconds. Add milk,
cook for a further 30 seconds and set aside.

• Pre-heat the toaster. Apply soft butter on one side of each bread
slice. Take two slices of bread, place a portion of the filling on the
buttered side and cover with the second slice, buttered
side down.

• Apply butter on top surface of the sandwich, turn over and place
sandwich in a toaster, now apply butter on the other surface.

• Close the toaster, and toast until golden brown.

• Garden sandwiches can be made with all kinds of bread – white,
brown, and multi-grain.
• This snack can be served for breakfast or as an afternoon snack.

• Remove butter from fridge half an hour before preparing to soften.

SAGO CUTLETS
Sabu Dana Vada

INGREDIENTS

½ cup Sago (*sabu dana*),
washed, soaked, drained, kept
covered for 8 hours
4 Potatoes, medium-sized boiled
(see p. 183), peeled, grated
2 Bread slices, wet, squeezed
(see p. 199)
2 tsp Ginger (*adrak*), chopped
½ tsp Green chilies, chopped
2 tbsp Cilantro (*dhaniya*) leaves,
chopped
¼ cup Peanuts (*moongphalli*),
skinned, coarsely ground
(see p. 185)
½ tsp Salt
Vegetable oil for deep-frying

METHOD

• Mix the grated potato with
sago, squeezed bread, ginger,
green chilies, cilantro leaves,
ground peanuts, and salt into
a smooth mixture.

• Divide the mixture equally
into 12-15 portions and
shape into round, flat cutlets.

• Heat 1"-deep oil in a shallow
pan; deep-fry the cutlets
in hot oil until light golden
brown and serve hot.

• Sago cutlets can be served with green chutney (see p. 154) and
sweet chutney (see p. 157).

• Do not fry more than 3-4 cutlets at a time to avoid breaking.
• Sago cutlets make an excellent party snack.

SPICY POTATO PATTIES
Chatpati Aloo Tikki

INGREDIENTS

10 Potatoes, boiled (see p. 183),
peeled, grated
2 Bread slices, wet, squeezed
(see p. 199)
1½ tbsp Cornstarch
½ tsp Salt
Vegetable oil for shallow-frying

For the filling:

1 cup Green peas (*hara mattar*),
boiled, ground coarsely in a food
processor
1 tbsp Vegetable oil
a pinch Asafetida (*hing*)
¾ tsp Cumin (*jeera*) seeds
1 tsp Ginger (*adrak*) paste (see
p. 191)
1 tsp Green chili paste (see p.
191)
1 tsp Red chili powder
½ tsp *Garam masala* (see p.
184)
½ tsp Mango powder (*amchur*)
1 tbsp Cilantro (*dhaniya*) leaves,
chopped
Salt to taste

METHOD

- **For the filling**, heat 1 tbsp
  oil in a pan for 30 seconds;
  add asafetida, cumin seeds,
  ginger paste, green chili paste,
  and ground green peas; mix.
  Add red chili powder, *garam
  masala*, mango powder,
  cilantro leaves, and salt to
  taste; cook on low heat for
  2 minutes. Remove and set
  filling aside.

- Mix the potato, squeezed
  bread, corn flour, and salt into

a smooth mixture.

- Divide the potato mixture
  into 20 equal-sized balls. Stuff
  each potato ball with 1 tsp
  pea filling and shape into a
  flat round patty.

- Shallow-fry the patties in hot
  oil until light golden brown.
  Serve immediately.

- Potato patties can be served with lunch and dinner as well as a
  snack.

- Serve the patties with sweet chutney (see p. 157), green chutney
  (see p. 154), and tomato sauce.

SPICY POTATO PRISMS
Samosa

INGREDIENTS

For the dough:

2½ cups All-purpose flour (*maida*)

½ tsp Salt

3 tbsp Clarified butter (*ghee*), melted

Lukewarm water to make the dough

Vegetable oil for deep-frying

For the stuffing:

4 Potatoes, medium-sized, boiled (see p. 183), peeled, coarsely mashed

1 tbsp Vegetable oil

a pinch Asafetida (*hing*)

1 tsp Cumin (*jeera*) seeds

1 tsp Ginger (*adrak*) paste (see p. 191)

½ tsp Green chili paste (see p. 191)

3 tsp Ground coriander (*dhaniya*)

1 tsp Mango powder (*amchur*)

1 tsp Red chili powder

½ tsp *Garam masala* (see p. 184)

Salt to taste

2 tbsp Cilantro (*dhaniya*) leaves, chopped

METHOD

- Sieve the flour and salt together. Add melted clarified butter and prepare a semi-hard dough with lukewarm water. Cover and set aside for 10 minutes.

- **For the stuffing**, heat 1 tbsp oil in a pan for 30 seconds; add asafetida, cumin seeds, ginger and green chili pastes, and mashed potato; mix well. Add ground coriander, mango powder, red chili powder, *garam* masala, salt to taste, and cilantro leaves; mix well. Cook on low heat for 5 minutes, turning occasionally. Remove and cool.

- Divide the dough equally into 20 balls. Roll each ball evenly with a rolling pin, into a disc of 5" diameter and cut in half.

- Apply water to each semi-circle and make a hollow cone.

- Fill each cone with potato stuffing and seal the ends.

- Heat 1"-deep oil in a shallow pan; deep-fry the prisms in medium-hot oil until light golden brown and serve hot.

- To avoid bubbles in the flour covering of the *samosa*, fry in lukewarm oil first then turn up the heat after 2 minutes and deep-fry until light golden brown.

- *Samosa* is an all-time favorite snack among adults and children alike.
- Serve with green chutney (see p. 154) and sweet chutney (see p. 157).

SAVORY RICE FLAKES
Poha

INGREDIENTS

1 cup Beaten rice (*chiwda*), washed, drained in a colander
1-2 tbsp Vegetable oil
¼ tsp Mustard seeds (*rai*)
2 tsp Ginger (*adrak*), chopped
1 tsp Green chilies, chopped
12 Curry leaves (*kadhi patta*)
1 tbsp Raisins (*kishmish*), chopped
2 tbsp Cashew nuts (*kaju*), chopped
¾ cup Green peas (*hara mattar*), boiled
Salt to taste
½ tsp Sugar
1 tsp Lemon (*nimbu*) juice
2 tbsp Cilantro (*dhaniya*) leaves, chopped

METHOD

• Heat 1-2 tbsp oil in a pan for 30 seconds; add mustard seeds, ginger, green chilies, curry leaves, raisins, and cashew nuts. Cook for 30 seconds. Add green peas and cook for a minute.

• Add washed and drained beaten rice, salt to taste, sugar, lemon juice, and cilantro leaves; mix well.

• Cook on low heat, covered, for 2 minutes. Serve hot.

• Savory rice flakes are mainly served as a breakfast dish.
• Roasted peanuts can be substituted for cashew nuts.

• It can also be served with toasted bread.

SAVORY SEMOLINA CAKES
Rawa Idli

Serves: 4-6

INGREDIENTS

1 cup Semolina (*rawa*), dry roasted (see p. 185)
1½ cups Yogurt (*dahi*), sour
1 tsp Salt
1½ tbsp Vegetable oil
2 tsp Bengal gram (*chana dal*), dehusked, split
2 tsp Black gram (*dhuli urad dal*), dehusked, split
1 tsp Mustard seeds (*rai*)
2 tsp Curry leaves (*kadhi patta*), chopped
1 tsp Baking soda
2 tbsp Cilantro (*dhaniya*) leaves, chopped
2 tsp Vegetable oil for greasing

METHOD

• Mix the roasted semolina with yogurt and salt to prepare a batter.

• Heat 1½ tbsp oil in a pan; add both the lentils and cook until light brown. Add mustard seeds and curry leaves; mix well. Remove and mix with the semolina batter. Add baking soda and stir in the batter. Mix well.

• Grease the semolina cake / *idli* stand with 2 tsp oil, add 1½ tbsp batter to each mold and steam for 8-10 minutes or until done (test with a toothpick).

• Remove the semolina cakes with the help of a knife.

• Serve hot with coconut chutney (see p. 156).

• Baking soda should be added in the end, to ensure that *idlis* are light.
• For better taste use slightly sour yogurt, preferably 1-2 days old.
• An *idli* stand is a stainless steel utensil with steaming compartments.

The stand is placed in a large vessel containing water to steam the semolina or rice cakes.

SPICY SEMOLINA
Rawa Upma

INGREDIENTS

1 cup Semolina (*rawa*)
2 tbsp Vegetable oil
1 cup Onions, cut into medium-sized cubes
2 tsp Ginger (*adrak*), chopped
1 Green chili, slit
2 tsp Bengal gram (*chana dal*), dehusked split
2 tsp Black gram (*dhuli urad dal*), dehusked, split
¾ tsp Mustard seeds (*rai*)
12 Curry leaves (*kadhi patta*)
2½ cups Water
Salt to taste
1 tbsp Clarified butter (*ghee*)
2 tbsp Cilantro (*dhaniya*) leaves, chopped
1 tbsp Lemon (*nimbu*) juice
2 tbsp Peanuts (*moongphalli*), fried

METHOD

- Heat 1½ tbsp oil in a pan for 30 seconds; add onions, ginger, and green chili. Cook until light brown. Add semolina and cook until light brown. Remove and keep aside.

- In the same pan, heat ½ tbsp oil; add the lentils and fry until light pink in color. Add mustard seeds and curry leaves; mix well.

- Add 2½ cups water and salt to taste and bring to a boil. Add roasted semolina, little by little, stirring constantly. Cook until semi-thick.

- Add clarified butter, cilantro leaves, lemon juice, and peanuts. Turn off the heat and leave covered for 2 minutes. Mix and serve hot.

- Spicy semolina is relished at breakfast or tea time with coconut chutney (see p. 156).
- The preparation of semolina with onion can be done in advance.

- Seasoning with lentils and mixing with water should be done just before serving.

VEGETABLE VERMICELLI
Sabzdar Sewai

INGREDIENTS

1 cup Vermicelli (*sewai*)
¼ tsp Clarified butter (*ghee*)
¼ cup Beans, cut diagonally into 1" pieces
¼ cup Carrot (*gajar*), cut diagonally into 1" pieces
2 tbsp Vegetable oil
½ tsp Mustard seeds (*rai*)
1 tsp Bengal gram (*chana dal*), dehusked, split
1 tsp Black gram (*dhuli urad dal*), dehusked, split
2 tsp Ginger (*adrak*), chopped
1 tsp Green chilies, chopped
15 Curry leaves (*kadhi patta*)
1 cup Onions, sliced
1 cup Water
Salt to taste
2 tsp Cilantro (*dhaniya*) leaves, chopped
1 tsp Lemon (*nimbu*) juice

METHOD

- Melt ¼ tsp clarified butter in a pan; add vermicelli and cook on low heat until light golden brown (see p. 185). Remove and keep aside.

- Boil 2½ cups water; add cut carrot and beans and cook for a minute. Remove and drain.

- Heat 2 tbsp oil in a pan for 30 seconds; add mustard seeds and both lentils, fry until light brown. Add ginger, green chilies, curry leaves, and onions; cook until light brown.

- Add roasted vermicelli, 1 cup water, and salt to taste. Mix well. Cook covered, on low heat, until the water evaporates.

- Add the vegetables, cilantro leaves, and lemon juice. Mix and serve hot.

- Cook vermicelli in a flat pan for better texture.
- Soak the lentils in ½ cup water to soften. Drain before use.

- Serve with coconut chutney (see p. 156) or green chutney (see p. 154).

SPICY INDIAN PUFFS
Pani Puri

INGREDIENTS

For the puffs (*puri*):

50 gm Semolina (*rawa*)

50 gm All-purpose flour (*maida*)

Water to make the dough

Vegetable oil for deep-frying

For the liquid filling:

2 Raw mangoes (*kairi*), medium-sized

2 cups Mint (*pudina*) leaves, chopped

1 tbsp Ginger (*adrak*), chopped

2 tsp Green chilies, chopped

4 cups Water

¼ tsp Asafetida (*hing*)

1 tsp *Garam masala* (see p. 184)

4 Cloves (*laung*), roasted, ground

2 tsp Roasted cumin (*jeera*) powder (see p. 184)

½ tsp Red chili powder

1 tbsp Lemon (*nimbu*) juice

Salt to taste

1 tsp Black salt (*kala namak*)

For the filling mixture:

1 cup Potatoes, boiled, chopped (see p. 183)

1 cup Horse gram (*kala chana*), boiled (see p. 192)

Salt, red chili powder, and cumin powder to taste

1 tbsp Cilantro (*dhaniya*) leaves, chopped

METHOD

- **For the puffs (*puri*)**, sieve the semolina and flour together and prepare a semi-hard dough with water. Cover and set aside for 15 minutes. Divide the dough equally into 50 balls and roll with a rolling pin into thin round discs of 1¼" diameter. Place the discs on a moistened cloth napkin and leave covered with another moistened cloth napkin for 30 minutes. Turn upside down holding the napkin edges.

- Heat 1"-deep oil in a shallow pan; deep-fry the discs in medium-hot oil, one at a time, until light golden brown. Remove, cool, and store in an airtight container for later use.

- **For the liquid filling**, pressure cook the mangoes with 2½ cups water to one whistle. Then simmer for 2 minutes. Remove and cool. Peel and mash the mangoes with the palm and discard seeds.

- Blend the mango pulp with mint, ginger, green chilies, and 4 cups water; strain. Add asafetida, *garam masala*, roasted clove powder, cumin powder, red chili powder, lemon juice, salt to taste, and black salt; stir well.

- **To serve**, mix together all the filling ingredients. Fill the puffs with 1 tsp filling mixture and pour liquid filling into the puff. Serve immediately.

- For a sweeter taste add 1 tsp sweet chutney (see p. 157) into the puff.

- *Pani puri* is a must for *chaat* parties.
- Ready-made puffs can often be bought from any Indian savory store.

- Mango can be replaced with 2 cups of tamarind water (see p. 83).
- These are also known as *gol gappa* in North India and *puchka* in Eastern India.

SPICY CHAAT BOWLS
Chaat Katori

INGREDIENTS
2 cups All-purpose flour (*maida*)
½ tsp Salt
1 tbsp Vegetable oil
½ tsp Carom (*ajwain*) seeds
Lukewarm water to make the dough
Vegetable oil for deep-frying

For the filling:
1¼ cups White peas (*safed mattar*), soaked for 6-8 hours, boiled (see p. 193)
2 Potatoes, medium-sized, boiled (see p. 183), peeled, chopped
1 cup Green chutney (see p. 154)
2 cups Sweet chutney (see p. 157)
2 cups Yogurt (*dahi*), beaten (see p. 198)
Salt to taste
Red chili powder and roasted cumin powder (see p. 184) to taste
Thin *sev* and Cilantro (*dhaniya*) leaves chopped for decoration
20 Steel molds (*katori*) (size 2¼")

METHOD

- Sieve the flour with salt. Add oil and carom seeds and prepare a hard dough with lukewarm water. Cover and set aside for 10 minutes. Divide the dough into 20 equal balls. Roll each ball evenly with a rolling pin, into a disc 4½" in diameter.

- Stick each disc on the outer surface of a mold (*katori*), crimp the edges and prick with a fork.

- Heat 1"-deep oil in a shallow pan; fry in medium-hot oil for 2 minutes.

- Gently pry away the steel molds from the flour base after 2 minutes. Continue to fry separated flour "bowl" (*chaat katori*) until light golden brown.

- To serve, take each flour bowl (*chaat katori*) and fill it with 1½ tbsp white peas, 1 tbsp chopped potatoes, 1 tsp green chutney, 2 tsp sweet chutney, and 1 tbsp beaten yogurt. Sprinkle with salt, red chili powder, and roasted cumin powder to taste and garnish with thin *sev* and cilantro leaves. Serve immediately.

- You may vary the quantities of green chutney and sweet chutney to taste.
- This can be served for an afternoon snack or at *chaat* parties.

- *Safed mattar* is also called *ragada* in Hindi.
- Remove the steel molds (*katori*) with the help of tong and spoon when the bowls are half done.

MAIN COURSES

YELLOW LENTIL
Arhar Dal

Serves: 4

INGREDIENTS

1 cup Yellow lentil (*arhar dal*), washed, soaked for 30 minutes
2 Tomatoes, medium-sized, 1 grated, 1 roasted, peeled, cut into cubes (see p. 186)
¾ tsp Salt
½ tsp Turmeric (*haldi*) powder
2 tsp Ginger (*adrak*), chopped
2 tbsp Cilantro (*dhaniya*) leaves, chopped

For the tempering:
1 tbsp Clarified butter (*ghee*)
a pinch Asafetida (*hing*)
1 tsp Cumin (*jeera*) seeds
½ tsp Red chili powder

METHOD

- Pressure cook the soaked lentil with 1½ cups water, salt, and turmeric powder to one whistle and simmer for 4 minutes.

- Open the lid when the pressure drops, add the grated and cubed tomato, ginger, and cilantro leaves; bring the mixture to a boil. Transfer to a serving bowl and season with the tempering.

- **For the tempering**, heat 1 tbsp clarified butter in a pan; add all the ingredients in the same order as mentioned (see p. 194). Remove and pour over the lentil. Serve hot.

- To give a fresh look to the lentil, always add the tempering just before serving.

- *Arhar dal* is also called *toor dal*, and is one of the most popular lentils used in Indian cuisine. It is the main ingredient of *sambar*.

BROWN LENTIL
Kale Masoor ki Dal

INGREDIENTS

1 cup Whole red lentil (*kale masoor*), washed, soaked for 30 minutes
Salt to taste
½ tsp Turmeric (*haldi*) powder
¼ tsp Sugar
¼ *Garam masala* (see p. 184)
¼ tsp Mango powder (*amchur*)
2 tsp Ginger (*adrak*), chopped
1 tbsp Cilantro (*dhaniya*) leaves, chopped

For the tempering:
1 tbsp Clarified butter (*ghee*)
a pinch Asafetida (*hing*)
¾ tsp Cumin (*jeera*) seeds
½ tsp Red chili powder

METHOD

- Pressure cook the soaked lentil with 2½ cups water, salt, and turmeric powder to one whistle, simmer for 10 minutes.

- Open the lid when the pressure drops. Add sugar, *garam masala*, mango powder, ginger, and cilantro leaves; bring the mixture to a boil. Transfer to a serving bowl and season with the tempering.

- **For the tempering,** heat 1 tbsp clarified butter in a pan; add all the ingredients mentioned in the same order (see p. 194). Remove and pour over the lentil. Serve hot.

- Lentils are normally served at lunch time with one or two dry vegetables.

TEMPERED MIXED LENTIL
Dal Tarka

INGREDIENTS

$1/_8$ cup Split green gram (*chilka moong dal*), washed, soaked for 30 minutes

$1/_3$ cup Bengal gram (*chana dal*), dehusked, soaked for 30 minutes

½ cup Red gram (*malka masoor*), washed, drained

Salt to taste

¼ tsp Turmeric (*haldi*) powder

2 Tomatoes, medium-sized, roasted, de-skinned, cut into small cubes (see p. 186)

2 tsp Ginger (*adrak*), chopped

1 tsp Green chilies, chopped

¼ tsp Mango powder (*amchur*)

¼ tsp *Garam masala* (see p. 184)

1 cup Fenugreek (*methi*) leaves, chopped, cooked (see p. 196)

2 tbsp Cilantro (*dhaniya*) leaves, chopped

For the tempering:

1 tbsp Clarified butter (*ghee*)

a pinch Asafetida (*hing*)

½ tsp Cumin (*jeera*) seeds

¼ tsp Red chili powder

METHOD

• Pressure cook the soaked lentils (see p. 192) with 2½ cups water, salt to taste, and turmeric powder to one whistle, simmer for 4 minutes.

• Open the lid when the pressure drops. Add chopped tomatoes, ginger, green chilies, mango powder, and *garam masala*; bring the mixture to a boil. Add cooked fenugreek and cook for a minute. Transfer to a serving dish and season with the tempering.

• **For the tempering**, heat 1 tbsp clarified butter in a pan; add all the ingredients mentioned in the same order (see p. 194). Remove and pour over the lentil. Serve hot.

• Red gram cooks very fast so avoid soaking it.

SPICED GREEN BANANAS IN YOGURT CURRY
Kele ki Kadi

INGREDIENTS

2 Green bananas (*kela*), medium-sized
1¼ cups Yogurt (*dahi*), sour
1½ tbsp Gram flour (*besan*)
1½ cups Water
2 tbsp Cilantro (*dhaniya*) leaves, chopped

For the basic seasoning:
2 tsp Clarified butter (*ghee*)
a pinch Asafetida (*hing*)
¼ tbsp Fenugreek seeds (*methi dana*)
¼ Cumin (*jeera*) seeds
4 Dry red chilies (*sookhi lal mirch*)
½ tsp Red chili powder
½ tsp Turmeric (*haldi*) powder

For the tempering:
1 tbsp Clarified butter
a pinch Asafetida
¼ tsp Mustard seeds (*rai*)
6 Curry leaves (*kadhi patta*)
¼ tsp Red chili powder

METHOD

- Pressure cook the bananas (see p. 183). Peel and cut into semi-circles.

- Mix the yogurt with gram flour and 1½ cups water and make a smooth paste. Set aside.

- **For the basic seasoning**, heat 2 tsp clarified butter in a pan for 30 seconds; add all the ingredients mentioned in the same order and mix.

- Add the cut bananas, yogurt mixture, and salt; bring to a boil, stirring constantly. Reduce heat and simmer for 10 minutes.

- Add cilantro leaves and transfer to a serving bowl and season with the tempering.

- **For the tempering**, heat 1 tbsp clarified butter in a pan; add all the ingredients mentioned in the same order (see p. 194). Pour over the prepared dish.

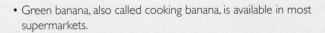

- Green banana, also called cooking banana, is available in most supermarkets.

- This dish can be served for both lunch and dinner.

DUMPLINGS IN SPICY YOGURT SAUCE
Kadi Pakodi

INGREDIENTS

For the gram flour balls (*pakodi*):
1 cup Gram flour (*besan*)
2 tsp Ginger (*adrak*), chopped
1 tsp Green chilies, chopped
Vegetable oil for shallow-frying

For the yogurt curry:
2 cups Yogurt (*dahi*), sour
½ cup Gram flour
3½ cups Water

For the basic seasoning:
1 tbsp Clarified butter
a pinch Asafetida (*hing*)
¼ tsp Fenugreek seeds (*methi dana*)
½ tsp Cumin (*jeera*) seeds
4 Dry red chilies (*sookhi lal mirch*)
1 tsp Turmeric (*haldi*) powder
½ tsp gm Red chili powder

For the tempering:
1 tbsp Clarified butter
a pinch Asafetida
½ tsp Cumin seeds
¼ tsp Red chili powder
1 tbsp Cilantro (*dhaniya*) leaves, chopped

• This recipe is very typical of Uttar Pradesh, a state in north India. *Kadi pakodi* is always served with steamed rice.

• It is often served as a family treat on Sundays.
• 2-day-old refrigerated yogurt is considered sour enough for this dish.

METHOD

- **For the gram flour balls (*pakodi*)**, prepare a semi-thick batter with gram flour and water. Add chopped ginger and green chilies. Beat until light and fluffy. (To test if the batter is fluffy drop ¼ tsp batter in ½ cup water, if batter floats it assures soft gram flour balls.)

- Heat ½"-deep oil in a shallow pan on medium heat; drop small portions of batter with your fingers and fry until light golden brown. Remove and immediately immerse in salted water; dip and remove. (For salted water, take 3¾ cups water and mix with 1½ tsp salt.)

- **For the yogurt curry**, mix the yogurt and gram flour with 3½ cups water to a smooth texture. Set aside.

- **For the basic seasoning**, heat 1 tbsp clarified butter in a pan; add all the ingredients mentioned in the same order.

- Add the yogurt mixture and salt to taste; bring to a boil. Add soaked gram flour balls and bring to a boil. Reduce heat and simmer for 15 minutes. Serve hot with the tempering.

- **For the tempering**, heat 1 tbsp clarified butter in a pan; add all the ingredients mentioned in the same order (see p. 194). Pour over the prepared dish.

- The process of dipping and removing the *pakodi* from water helps to remove the excess oil but still keeps it firm.

BENGAL GRAM WITH BOTTLE GOURD
Lauki Chane ki Dal

INGREDIENTS

¾ cup Bengal gram (*chana dal*),
de-husked, washed, soaked for
30 minutes
1½ cups Bottle gourd (*lauki*),
peeled
2 tsp Ginger (*adrak*), chopped
1 Green chili, slit
Salt to taste
½ tsp Turmeric (*haldi*) powder
2 tbsp Cilantro (*dhaniya*) leaves,
chopped
2 tsp Lemon (*nimbu*) juice

For the tempering:
1 tbsp Clarified butter (*ghee*)
a pinch Asafetida (*hing*)
½ tsp Cumin (*jeera*) seeds
½ tsp Red chili powder

METHOD

- Peel and cut bottle gourd into 1" cubes.

- Pressure cook the soaked lentil, bottle gourd, ginger, green chili, salt, and turmeric powder with 2 cups water, to one whistle; simmer for 10 minutes.

- Open the lid when the pressure drops. Add cilantro leaves and bring the mixture to a boil. Reduce heat and simmer for 2 minutes. Add lemon juice and mix well. Transfer to a serving bowl and season with the tempering.

- **For the tempering**, heat 1 tbsp clarified butter in a pan; add all the ingredients in the same order mentioned (see p. 194). Pour over the prepared lentil.

- Avoid adding lemon juice while cooking, as the preparation may get bitter.
- Bengal gram and bottle gourd complement each other.

LENTIL DUMPLINGS & SPINACH IN YOGURT SAUCE
Magori Palak ki Kadi

Serves: 4-6

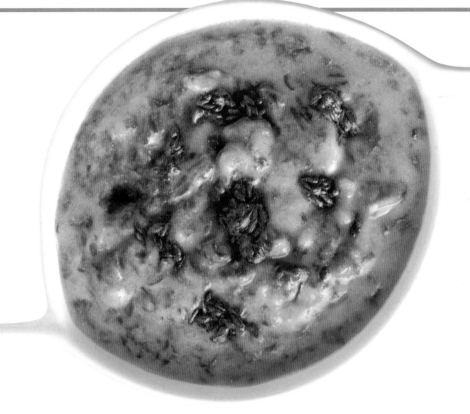

INGREDIENTS

1 cup Sun-dried green gram
dumplings (*magori*) (see p. 185)
2 cups Spinach (*palak*), chopped,
cooked (see p. 196)
Vegetable oil for deep-frying
1½ cups Yogurt (*dahi*), sour
2 tbsp Gram flour (*besan*)
1 tsp Ginger (*adrak*) paste
(see p. 191)
1 tsp Green chili paste
(see p. 191)
1½ cups Water

For the seasoning:
½ tbsp Clarified butter (*ghee*)
a pinch Asafetida (*hing*)
1 tsp Cumin (*jeera*) seeds
¾ tsp Turmeric (*haldi*) powder
½ tsp Red chili powder

For the tempering:
1 tbsp Clarified butter
a pinch Asafetida
¼ tsp Cumin seeds
¼ tsp Red chili powder

METHOD

- Heat ½"-deep oil in a shallow pan; deep-fry the *magori* in medium-hot oil until light golden brown. Remove, crush them lightly and set aside.

- Mix yogurt, gram flour, ginger paste, and green chili paste with water to a smooth paste; set aside.

- **For the seasoning**, heat the pressure cooker for 30 seconds; add ½ tbsp clarified butter and the remaining ingredients in the same order; mix. Add fried and crushed *magori*; mix. Add 1½ cups water and ¼ tsp salt; cook to one whistle, and simmer for 5 minutes. Turn off the heat.

- Open the lid when the pressure drops. Add yogurt mixture and salt to taste; bring to a boil. Reduce heat and simmer for 10 minutes.

- Add cooked spinach and bring to a boil. Remove and transfer to a serving bowl and season with the tempering.

- **For the tempering**, heat 1 tbsp clarified butter in a pan; add all the ingredients in the same order mentioned (see p. 194). Pour over the prepared dish.

- *Magoris* are prepared by soaking and grinding split green gram, shaping into small dumplings and then drying them in the sun. They are available in most Indian food stores.

- Mix spinach just before serving as this gives a fresh appetizing look.
- Mash the cooked spinach before adding.

SPLIT GREEN LENTIL WITH SPINACH
Moong Dal Palak

INGREDIENTS

1 cup Green gram (*moong dal*), washed, soaked for 15 minutes
1½ cups Spinach (*palak*), chopped, cooked
(see p. 196)
¼ tsp Clarified butter (*ghee*)
Salt to taste
½ tsp Turmeric (*haldi*) powder
1½ tsp Ginger (*adrak*), chopped
1 Tomato, medium-sized, chopped

For the tempering:
1 tbsp Clarified butter
a pinch Asafetida (*hing*)
1 tsp Cumin (*jeera*) seeds
2 Cloves (*laung*)
¼ tsp Black pepper (*kali mirch*)

METHOD

• Heat the pressure cooker for 30 seconds; add ¼ tsp clarified butter, green gram, salt to taste, turmeric powder, ginger, tomato, cooked spinach, and 2 cups water. Cook to one whistle, remove from heat.

• Open the lid when the pressure drops. Bring the mixture to a boil. Transfer to a serving dish and season with the tempering.

• **For the tempering**, heat 1 tbsp clarified butter in the pan; add all the ingredients in the same order mentioned (see p. 194). Pour over the lentil. Serve hot.

• Green gram cooks very fast. To avoid over-cooking, the pressure has to be monitored.

• It can be served to those who require an iron-rich diet.

CURRIED KIDNEY BEANS
Rajmah

Serves: 4-6

INGREDIENTS

1 cup Kidney beans (*rajmah*), washed, soaked for 8 hours
½ tsp Salt
1 tsp Turmeric (*haldi*) powder (¾ + ¼)
3 tbsp Vegetable oil
2 Bay leaves (*tej patta*)
2 Black cardamom (*badi elaichi*), crushed
3 Onions, medium-sized, grated
2 tsp Ginger (*adrak*) paste (see p. 191)
½ tsp Green chili paste (see p. 191)
¼ tsp Garlic (*lasan*) paste (see p. 191)
¾ tsp Red chili powder
4 Tomatoes, large, liquidized (see p. 187)
½ tsp *Garam masala* (see p. 184)
2 tbsp Cilantro (*dhaniya*) leaves, chopped

METHOD

- Pressure cook the soaked beans with 4½ cups water, salt, and ¼ tsp turmeric powder to one whistle. Reduce heat and simmer for 30 minutes. Turn off the heat.

- Heat 3 tbsp oil in a pan for 30 seconds; add bay leaves, black cardamom, onions, ginger, green chili and garlic pastes; fry until light golden brown. Add ¾ tsp turmeric powder and red chili powder; mix.

- Add liquidized tomato and fry until oil separates.

- Add cooked kidney beans along with the water and salt to taste; bring to a boil. Reduce heat and simmer for 10 minutes.

- Add cilantro leaves and *garam masala*. Turn off the heat. Serve hot.

- Curried kidney beans tastes best with steamed rice.
- This is a popular north Indian dish.
- 2 tsp clarified butter can also be added to the dish to enhance the flavor.

- Beans are available in two colors, light brown and dark brown. The dark brown beans take 10 minutes more to pressure cook than the light brown beans.

FENUGREEK FLAVORED LENTIL
Urad Chana aur Methi Dal

INGREDIENTS

½ cup Split black gram (*dhuli urad dal*), dehusked
¹/₃ cup Bengal gram (*chana dal*), dehusked, split
Salt to taste
¾ tsp Turmeric (*haldi*) powder
2 tsp Ginger (*adrak*), chopped
1 tsp Green chilies, chopped
1 cup Fenugreek (*methi*) leaves, chopped
1 tsp Clarified butter (*ghee*)
3 Tomatoes, medium-sized, liquidized (see p. 187)
1½ cups Water

For the tempering:
1 tbsp Clarified butter
a pinch Asafetida (*hing*)
1 tsp Cumin (*jeera*) seeds
½ tsp Red chili powder

METHOD

- Wash and soak both the lentils together for 30 minutes. Pressure cook with salt to taste, turmeric powder, ginger, green chilies, and 1½ cups water to one whistle. Reduce heat and simmer for 4 minutes. Turn off the heat.

- Heat the pan for 30 seconds; add fenugreek leaves and cook covered for 30 seconds. Set aside.

- Heat 1 tsp clarified butter in a pan for 30 seconds; add liquidized tomato and salt to taste; cook for 2 minutes on medium heat. Remove and set aside.

- Add cooked fenugreek and tomato to the cooked lentil and bring the mixture to a boil. Remove and transfer to a serving bowl and season with tempering.

- **For the tempering,** heat 1 tbsp clarified butter in a pan; add all the ingredients in the same order mentioned (see p. 194). Pour over the lentil. Serve hot.

- Ensure that the tempering does not burn. To keep this from happening remove the pan from the heat after adding asafetida and cumin seeds. Add red chili powder later.

SPICY GREEN LENTIL
Sabut Moong ki Dal

INGREDIENTS

1 cup Whole green gram (*sabut moong dal*), washed, soaked for 30 minutes
¾ tsp Turmeric (*haldi*) powder
Salt to taste
1 tbsp Ginger (*adrak*) chopped
1 Green chili, slit
½ cup Tomatoes, grated (see p. 186)
½ tsp Mango powder (*amchur*)
½ tsp Sugar
¼ tsp *Garam masala* (see p. 184)
2 tbsp Cilantro (*dhaniya*) leaves, chopped

For the tempering:

1½ tbsp Clarified butter (*ghee*)
a pinch Asafetida (*hing*)
1 tsp Cumin (*jeera*) seeds
¾ tsp Red chili powder

METHOD

• Pressure cook the soaked lentil with 3 cups water, turmeric powder, salt, ginger, and green chili to one whistle. Reduce heat and simmer for 12 minutes. Turn off the heat.

• Open the lid when the pressure drops. Add grated tomato, mango powder, sugar, *garam masala,* and cilantro leaves; bring the mixture to a boil. Remove and transfer to a serving dish. Season with the tempering.

• **For the tempering**, heat 1½ tbsp clarified butter in a pan; add all the ingredients mentioned in the same order (see p. 194). Remove and pour over the lentil. Serve hot.

• This dish can be served with *besan methi roti* (see p. 138) and *khasta roti* (see p. 139).

• It is high in protein.
• Soaking the lentil for 30 minutes helps them to cook faster.

POTATOES AND PEPPER
Aloo Shimla Mirch

INGREDIENTS
2 Potatoes, medium-sized,
boiled (see p. 183) peeled, cut
lengthwise into fingers
1 Pepper (*Shimla mirch*),
medium-sized, cut lengthwise
into fingers
1½ tbsp Vegetable oil
a pinch Asafetida (*hing*)
½ tsp Cumin (*jeera*) seeds
2 tsp Gram flour (*besan*)
2 tsp Ground coriander
(*dhaniya*)
½ tsp Red chili powder
Salt to taste

METHOD
- Heat 1 tbsp oil in a pan for
  30 seconds; add asafetida,
  cumin seeds, and gram flour;
  cook for 10 seconds.

- Add cut pepper and cook for
  a minute. Add cut potatoes,
  cilantro powder, red chili
  powder, and salt to taste;
  cook on low heat for 2
  minutes, stirring occasionally.
  Serve hot.

- Gram flour gives a unique flavor to this dish.
- All varieties of bell peppers can be used.

TAMARIND FLAVORED POTATOES
Imli Aloo

Serves: 4-6

INGREDIENTS

6 Potatoes, medium-sized,
boiled (see p. 183), peeled, cut
into 1" cubes
2 tbsp Vegetable oil
a pinch Asafetida (*hing*)
1 tsp Cumin (*jeera*) seeds
¼ tsp Fenugreek seeds
(*methi dana*)
¼ tsp Fennel (*saunf*) seeds
4 Dry red chilies (*sookhi lal
mirch*)
1 tbsp Tamarind (*imli*) water
(see below)
3 tsp Ground coriander
(*dhaniya*)
1 tsp Red chili powder
½ tsp *Garam masala*
(see p. 184)
½ tsp *Chaat masala*
½ tsp Mint (*pudina*) powder
(see p. 11)
3 tbsp Cilantro (*dhaniya*) leaves,
chopped
Salt to taste

METHOD

- Heat 2 tbsp oil in a pan for
  30 seconds; add asafetida,
  cumin seeds, fenugreek seeds,
  fennel seeds, dry red chilies
  and tamarind water; cook for
  30 seconds. Add potatoes
  and mix well.

- Add ground coriander, red
  chili powder, *garam masala,
  chaat masala*, mint powder,
  cilantro leaves, and salt.
  Mix well. Cook on low
  heat for 5 minutes, stirring
  occasionally. Serve hot.

- *Imli aloo* can also be enjoyed as an appetizer as well.
- Soak 1 tbsp tamarind in ½ cup hot water for 30 minutes; mash and strain into a bowl. Discard the seeds and use the tamarind water as required.

POTATOES AND PEAS
Sukhe Aloo Mattar

INGREDIENTS

4 Potatoes, medium-sized, boiled (see p. 183), peeled, cut into 1" cubes

½ cup Green peas (*hara mattar*), boiled

2 tbsp Vegetable oil

a pinch Asafetida (*hing*)

1 tsp Cumin (*jeera*) seeds

¾ tsp Ginger (*adrak*) paste (see p. 191)

¼ tsp Turmeric (*haldi*) powder

½ tsp Red chili powder

2 Tomatoes, medium-sized, grated (see p. 186)

2 tsp Ground coriander (*dhaniya*)

¼ tsp *Garam masala* (see p. 184)

2 tbsp Cilantro (*dhaniya*) leaves, chopped

¼ tsp Cumin seeds

Salt and black pepper (*kali mirch*) to taste

METHOD

- Heat 1½ tbsp oil in a pan for 30 seconds; add asafetida, cumin seeds, ½ tsp ginger paste, turmeric powder, red chili powder, and grated tomato; cook until oil separates. Add cut potatoes and mix well.

- Add cilantro powder, salt to taste, *garam masala*, and cilantro leaves; cook for 5 minutes on low heat, stirring occasionally. Set aside.

- Heat ½ tbsp oil in a pan for 30 seconds; add cumin seeds, ¼ tsp ginger paste, green peas, salt and black pepper to taste; cook on low heat for 2 minutes.

- Mix with prepared potatoes. Serve hot.

- To retain the green color of the peas, it is advised to cook them separately from potatoes.

- Overcooking the greens generally changes their color.

SESAME POTATOES
Til Aloo

Serves: 10-12

INGREDIENTS

20 Baby potatoes, washed, wiped, make a cross with a sharp knife
2 tsp White sesame (*til*) seeds
2 tbsp Vegetable oil
½ tsp Cumin (*jeera*) seeds
½ tsp Ginger (*adrak*) paste (see p. 191)
½ tsp Green chili paste (see p. 191)
1 tsp Mint (*pudina*) paste
a pinch Asafetida (*hing*)
½ tsp *Chaat masala*
2 tbsp Cilantro (*dhaniya*) leaves, chopped

For the stuffing: mix and set aside

2 tsp Ground coriander (*dhaniya*)
¾ tsp Red chili powder
1 tsp Mango powder (*amchur*)
½ tsp *Garam masala* (see p. 184)
Salt to taste

METHOD

• Heat the pan for 30 seconds; add sesame seeds and roast on low heat, stirring constantly, until light brown. Set aside.

• Place the potatoes in a container inside the pressure cooker filled with 1½ cups water, and cook to one whistle. Reduce heat and simmer for 4 minutes. Remove and cool.

• Fill the boiled potatoes with the stuffing *masala*.

• Heat 2 tbsp oil in a pan for

30 seconds; add cumin seeds, ginger paste, green chili paste, mint paste, stuffed potatoes, and *chaat masala*; cook on medium heat for 2 minutes, stirring constantly.

• Add cilantro leaves and roasted sesame seeds; mix well. Serve hot.

• Instead of pressure cooking, potatoes can also be baked at 400°F for 20-25 minutes or until soft, or they can be cooked in a microwave.
• Roasted sesame seeds give a nice crunchy element to this dish..

MINTY POTATOES
Pudina Aloo

Serves: 4-6

INGREDIENTS

10 Baby potatoes, boiled, peeled (see p. 183)
1½ tbsp Vegetable oil
a pinch Asafetida (*hing*)
½ tsp Cumin (*jeera*) seeds
1½ tsp Ginger (*adrak*) paste (see p. 191)
½ tbsp Green chili paste (see p. 191)
1 tsp Mint (*pudina*) paste
2 tsp Ground coriander (*dhaniya*)
¾ tsp Red chili powder
½ tsp Mango powder (*amchur*)
1 tsp Mint powder (see p. 11)
¼ tsp *Chaat masala*
¼ tsp *Garam masala* (see p. 184)
3 tbsp Mint, chopped
2 tbsp Cilantro (*dhaniya*) leaves, chopped
Salt to taste

METHOD

• Heat 1½ tbsp oil in a pan for 30 seconds; add asafetida, cumin seeds, ginger paste, green chili paste, and mint paste; cook for 10 seconds.

• Add potatoes and mix well. Add ground coriander; red chili powder, mango powder, mint powder, *chaat masala,* and *garam masala*; cook on low heat for 5 minutes, turning occasionally.

• Add mint, cilantro leaves and salt; mix and cook for a minute. Serve hot.

• The combination of dried and fresh mint paste makes this dish delicious.

CUMIN POTATOES
Jeera Aloo

INGREDIENTS

4 Potatoes, medium-sized, boiled (see p. 183), peeled, cut into 1" cubes
1 ½ tbsp Vegetable oil
a pinch Asafetida (*hing*)
½ tsp Cumin (*jeera*) seeds
2 tsp Ground coriander (*dhaniya*)
½ tsp Red chili powder
½ tsp Mango powder (*amchur*)
Salt to taste
2 tbsp Cilantro (*dhaniya*) leaves, chopped

METHOD

- Heat 1 ½ tbsp oil in a pan for 30 seconds; add asafetida and cumin seeds.

- Add cubed potatoes, ground coriander, red chili powder, mango powder, and salt; mix well. Cook on low heat for 5 minutes, stirring occasionally.

- Add cilantro leaves and cook for 30 seconds more. Serve hot.

- Cumin Potatoes is a popular dish. It is quick to prepare and can be served with any meal.

CAULIFLOWER AND POTATOES
Gobi Aloo

INGREDIENTS

1 Cauliflower (*phool gobi*), medium-sized, cut into 1½" florets
2 Potatoes, medium-sized, peeled, cut lengthwise into ½" pieces
1½ tbsp Vegetable oil
a pinch Asafetida (*hing*)
½ tsp Cumin (*jeera*) seeds
2 tsp Ginger (*adrak*), chopped
1 tsp Green chilies, chopped
¼ tsp Turmeric (*haldi*) powder
½ tsp Red chili powder
Salt to taste
½ tsp *Garam masala* (see p. 184)
¼ tsp Mango powder (*amchur*)
1 tbsp Cilantro (*dhaniya*) leaves, chopped

METHOD

- Heat 1½ tbsp oil in a heavy-bottom saucepan for 30 seconds; add asafetida, cumin seeds, ginger, chilies, turmeric powder, and red chili powder; mix.

- Add cut potatoes, cauliflower, salt, and ½ cup water. Cook, covered, on high heat, stirring occasionally, until the water dries up or the potatoes are cooked.

- Add *garam masala*, mango powder, and cilantro leaves; mix well. Serve hot.

- Cut potatoes should be kept in water otherwise they turn brown.
- This dish can be served for both lunch and dinner.

- If water dries up before the potatoes are done, it is advised to cook for 5 more minutes, covered, on low heat.

SPICY COLOCASIA
Sookhi Arvi

INGREDIENTS

1 cup Colocasia (*arvi*)
1½ tbsp Mustard oil / Vegetable oil
a pinch Asafetida (*hing*)
½ tsp Carom (*ajwain*) seeds
2 tsp Ground coriander (dhaniya)
½ tsp Red chili powder
¼ tsp Mango powder (*amchur*)
Salt to taste
2 tbsp Cilantro (*dhaniya*) leaves, chopped.

METHOD

- Pressure cook the colocasia with water to one whistle. Cool and drain.

- Peel and press colocasia within the palm. Set aside.

- Heat 1½ tbsp oil in a pan for 30 seconds; add asafetida, carom seeds, and colocasia; mix well.

- Add cilantro powder, red chili powder, mango powder, and salt. Cook on low heat for 5 minutes, stirring occasionally. Add cilantro leaves; mix. Serve hot.

- Colocasia is sticky by nature so avoid over-boiling.

- In north India, only a few dishes are cooked in mustard oil for its unique flavor.

ROASTED SPICED EGGPLANT
Baingan Bharta

Serves: 4-6

INGREDIENTS

1 Eggplant (*baingan*), large, make 4 1" deep slits
2 tbsp Vegetable oil +
1 tsp for applying
1 Onion, large, cut into medium-sized cubes
1½ tsp Ginger (*adrak*), chopped
1 tsp Green chilies, chopped
½ cup Green peas (*hara mattar*), boiled
Salt to taste
2 Tomatoes, medium-sized, 1 grated (see p. 186), 1 chopped into 8 pieces
¼ tsp Turmeric (*haldi*) powder
½ tsp Red chili powder
1 tbsp Cilantro (*dhaniya*) leaves, chopped

METHOD

• Apply 1 tsp oil to the outer surface of the eggplant. Roast over the flame until soft. Cool, peel, and mash. Set aside.

• Heat 1 tbsp oil in a pan; add onion, ginger, and green chilies; cook until light brown. Add green peas and salt to taste; cook for a minute. Add cut tomato and cook for 30 seconds. Remove.

• Heat 1 tbsp oil in the same pan; add turmeric powder, red chili powder, and grated tomato; cook for a minute. Add mashed eggplant and salt to taste; cook until semi-thick.

• Add the onion mixture and cilantro leaves; mix lightly for a minute. Serve hot.

• Applying oil to the outer surface of the eggplant helps to remove the skin easily.
• Roasting the eggplant enhances the flavor of the dish.

CRISPY EGGPLANT
Chatpate Baingan

INGREDIENTS

1 Eggplant (*baingan*), medium, cut into ¼"-thick slices
½ tsp Salt
½ tsp Turmeric (*haldi*) powder
3-4 tbsp Vegetable oil
Chaat masala and Cilantro (*dhaniya*) leaves, chopped

For coating the eggplant: mix and set aside
2 tbsp Wheat flour (*atta*)
½ tsp Salt
½ tsp Red chili powder
2 tsp Sesame (*til*) seeds
½ tsp Ground fennel (*saunf*)
¼ tsp *Garam masala* (see p. 184)

METHOD

- Sprinkle ½ tsp salt and ½ tsp turmeric powder on both sides of the eggplant and leave aside for 10 minutes. Use later for coating.

- Coat each slice of eggplant with coating mixture, on both sides, evenly.

- Heat 2 tbsp oil in a non-stick pan for 30 seconds; add 5-6 coated eggplant slices and cook until light golden brown on both sides, adding more oil if required. Repeat with the remaining slices.

- Serve hot, sprinkled with *chaat masala* and cilantro leaves.

- Crispy eggplant can be prepared for any meal.
- Sprinkling salt and turmeric powder on the eggplant slices extracts water, and hence aids in binding the coating to the eggplant.

OKRA WITH PEARL ONIONS
Bhindi aur Chhote Pyaz

INGREDIENTS

1 cup Okra (*bhindi*), remove
head and tail, cut diagonally in
¾" pieces
½ cup Baby onions, peeled
2 tbsp Vegetable oil
Salt to taste
1 tbsp Cilantro (*dhaniya*) leaves,
chopped
¼ tsp Sugar
2 Green chilies, medium-sized,
cut diagonally
¼ tsp Ground black pepper
(*kali mirch*)

METHOD

- Heat 1 tbsp oil in a pan for 30 seconds; add the onions and fry until light brown. Add salt and cilantro leaves; mix and set aside.

- Heat 1 tbsp oil in the same pan for 30 seconds; add okra, salt, sugar, and green chilies. Cover and cook on low heat until soft.

- Add black pepper and onion mixture; cook for a minute. Remove and transfer to a serving dish.

- Adding ¼ tsp sugar while cooking okra helps to retain the green color.

STUFFED OKRA
Bharwa Bhindi

INGREDIENTS

1 cup Okra (*bhindi*), washed, wiped dry with a clean napkin

For the stuffing:

½ tsp Turmeric (*haldi*) powder

2 tsp Ground coriander (*dhaniya*)

1 tsp Red chili powder

2 tsp Ground fennel (*saunf*)

¾ tsp Mango powder (*amchur*)

Salt to taste

For the seasoning:

2½ tbsp Vegetable oil

a pinch Asafetida (*hing*)

1 tsp Cumin (*jeera*) seeds

METHOD

- Cut the top and bottom of the okra and slit vertically with a sharp knife, keeping the shape intact.

- Mix the stuffing ingredients together; fill each okra evenly.

- Heat 2½ tbsp oil in a pan for 30 seconds; add asafetida, cumin seeds, and stuffed okra; Cover and cook, on low heat, stirring occasionally until the ends of the okra have softened. Serve hot.

- Select tender okra for better flavor.
- While cooking greens or any green vegetables, remove them from the pan as soon as they are cooked and cover them with a cloth instead of a lid to retain the green color.

BEANS WITH BABY CORN
Beans aur Chotte Bhutte

INGREDIENTS

1 cup Green beans, cut diagonally to 1" pieces
12 Baby corn (*bhutta*), cut diagonally to 1" pieces
¼ tsp Sugar
1 tbsp Vegetable oil
2 tsp Black gram (*dhuli urad dal*), de-husked, soaked for 15 minutes
2 tsp Bengal gram (*chana dal*), de-husked, soaked for 15 minutes
½ tsp Mustard seeds (*rai*)
¼ tsp Ginger (*adrak*) paste (see p. 191)
¼ tsp Garlic (*lasan*) paste (see p. 191)
2 Dry red chilies (*sookhi lal mirch*)
15 Curry leaves (*kadhi patta*)
Salt to taste
¼ tsp Black pepper (*kali mirch*)
2 tbsp Coconut (*nariyal*), grated

METHOD

- Boil 3½ cups water; add ¼ tsp sugar and beans; cook for 4 minutes. Drain.

- Boil 2½ cups water; add baby corn and cook for a minute. Drain.

- Heat 1 tbsp oil in a pan; add the lentils and cook for 30 seconds. Add mustard seeds, ginger-garlic paste, dry red chilies, and curry leaves; mix well.

- Add beans, baby corn, salt, and black pepper; cook for a minute. Add 1 tbsp grated coconut and mix.

- Remove and serve hot garnished with remaining coconut.

- This is a quick vegetable dish to prepare.
- Soaking helps the lentils to remain soft even after cooking.

BABY CORN AND PEPPER
Mazedaar Shimla Mirch aur Chhote Bhutte

Serves: 4-6

INGREDIENTS

30 Baby corn (*bhutta*), tender,
cut diagonally to 1" pieces
1 Pepper (*Shimla mirch*),
medium-sized, cut diagonally to
1" pieces
½ tbsp Corn flour
½ tbsp Gram flour (*besan*)
¾ tsp Red chili powder
(½ + ¼)
½ tsp *Garam masala* (¼ + ¼)
(see p. 184)
¼ tsp Mango powder (*amchur*)
1 tbsp Milk
Vegetable oil for cooking and
deep-frying
2 tbsp Onion, chopped
1 tsp Garlic (*lasan*) paste
(see p. 191)
½ tsp Green chili paste
(see p. 191)
Salt and black pepper
(*kali mirch*) to taste
2 tsp Honey
½ cup Scallions
(*hara pyaz*), chopped

METHOD

- Sprinkle ½ tbsp corn flour and ½ tbsp gram flour over the baby corn. Add ½ tsp red chili powder, ¼ tsp *garam masala*, mango powder, and milk; mix and leave aside for a minute.

- Heat 1"-deep oil in a shallow pan; deep-fry the baby corn mixed with spices in medium-hot oil for 2 minutes; set aside.

- Heat 1 tbsp oil in a pan for 30 seconds; add onion, garlic and green chili pastes; cook for a minute. Add pepper and cook for 30 seconds.

- Add fried baby corn, salt, black pepper, honey, ¼ tsp red chili powder, and ¼ tsp *garam masala*; mix well. Add scallions; mix. Serve hot.

- Mix the baby corn with the vegetables just before serving for better flavor and texture.

- This is a popular party dish.
- Cut corn should measure up to 2 cups and pepper up to ¾ cup.

CORN A LA CILANTRO
Dhaniyawale Makai ke Dane

INGREDIENTS

1 cup Sweet corn (*makai*)
Vegetable oil for cooking
1 Onion, medium-sized, chopped
1 tsp Ginger (*adrak*), chopped
¼ tsp Garlic (*lasan*), chopped
¼ tsp Red chili powder
2 tsp Ground cilantro (*dhaniya*)
4 Tomatoes, medium-sized, 3 roasted and cut into cubes, 1 grated (see p. 186)
¼ tsp Sugar
Salt to taste
¼ tsp *Garam masala* (see p. 184)
2 tbsp Cilantro (*dhaniya*) leaves, chopped

METHOD

- Heat 2 tsp oil in a pan for 30 seconds, add sweet corn and cook for 2 minutes on medium heat, stirring occasionally. Remove and set aside.

- Heat 1 tbsp oil in the same pan for 30 seconds, add onion, ginger, and garlic; sauté until light pink. Add red chili powder, and cilantro mix. Add cut and grated tomatoes and sugar, cook until semi-thick.

- Add cooked corn, salt to taste, *garam masala*, and cilantro leaves; cook for a minute on high heat. Serve hot.

- Fresh cilantro leaves enhances the flavor of this dish.

BEAN SPROUTS WITH BELL PEPPER
Ankurit Moong aur Shimla Mirch

INGREDIENTS

2 cups Bean sprouts
1 Bell pepper (*Shimla mirch*), medium-sized, cut diagonally to 1" pieces
2 Tomatoes, medium-sized
½ Yogurt (*dahi*)
2 tsp Gram flour (*besan*)
1 tbsp Vegetable oil
a pinch Asafetida (*hing*)
½ tsp Cumin (*jeera*) seeds
½ tsp Ginger (*adrak*) paste (see p. 191)
¼ tsp Green chili paste (see p. 191)
¼ tsp Turmeric (*haldi*) powder
¼ tsp Red chili powder
Salt to taste
¼ tsp *Garam masala* (see p. 184)
1 tbsp Cilantro (*dhaniya*) leaves, chopped

METHOD

- Boil 3½ cups water; add bean sprouts and cook for 1½ minutes. Drain. Roast the tomatoes (see p. 186), peel and cut diagonally to 1" pieces.

- Mix yogurt with 2 tsp gram flour to a smooth paste.

- Heat 1 tbsp oil in a pan; add asafetida, cumin seeds, ginger and green chili pastes. Add turmeric powder, red chili powder, and yogurt mixture; cook for 2 minutes.

- Add sprouts and salt; cook until semi-thick.

- Add pepper and tomatoes; cook for 2 minutes. Add *garam masala* and mix well. Serve hot garnished with cilantro leaves.

- Cut pepper should measure up to ½ cup and tomatoes up to 1 cup.
- Yogurt and gram flour should be mixed properly, otherwise the mixture may curdle.
- Sprouts are high in protein.
- Boiled sprouts mixed with tomato and salt can also be served for breakfast.

STUFFED GREEN CHILIES
Bharwa Mirchi

Serves: 6-8

INGREDIENTS

8 Light green chilies (*mirchi*)
1½ tbsp Mustard (*sarson*)/
Vegetable oil
a pinch Asafetida (*hing*)
¼ tsp Cumin (*jeera*) seeds
¼ tsp Carom (*ajwain*) seeds
2 tsp Gram flour (*besan*)

For the stuffing: mix and set aside

4 Potatoes, medium-sized, boiled
(see p. 183), peeled, grated
1½ tsp Ground fennel (*saunf*)
½ tsp Ground cilantro (*dhaniya*)
½ tsp Mango powder (*amchur*)
¼ tsp *Garam masala*
(see p. 184)
¼ tsp Red chili powder
1 tbsp Cilantro (*dhaniya*) leaves,
chopped
Salt to taste

METHOD

- Slit the green chilies vertically
  with a sharp knife, keeping the
  shape intact, and deseed.

- Tightly stuff the chilies with
  the stuffing mixture tightly. Cut into 2 pieces.

- Heat 1½ tbsp oil in a pan for 30 seconds; add asafetida, cumin
  seeds, carom seeds, and gram flour; cook for 10 seconds. Add
  stuffed chilies and cook on high heat for 2 minutes, stirring
  constantly. Serve hot.

- Stuffed green chilies are spicy in taste.
- The stuffing can also vary, for example: grated *masala* cottage cheese (see p. 189) and *sookhi moong dal* (see p. 50) mixture can also be used.

BABY CARROTS WITH FENUGREEK LEAVES
Gajar Methi

Serves: 4-6

INGREDIENTS
½ lb Baby carrots (*gajar*), peeled
2 cups Fenugreek (*methi*) leaves, chopped, washed, dried over napkins
1½ tbsp Vegetable oil
a pinch Asafetida (*hing*)
½ tsp Cumin (*jeera*) seeds
Salt to taste
¼ tsp Sugar
½ tsp Red chili powder
1 tsp Ground cilantro (*dhaniya*)

METHOD
- Heat 1½ tbsp oil in a pan; add asafetida, cumin seeds, and carrots; sauté for a minute. Add ½ cup water, salt to taste, and sugar; cook covered on low heat until done.

- Add red chili powder and cilantro; cook for 30 seconds.

- Add fenugreek leaves and cook on high heat for a minute; toss frequently. Serve hot.

- When the carrot ends are soft, the carrots are done.
- Both orange and red carrots can be used.
- Normally in India, red carrots are available during winter.
- Carrots are rich in vitamin A.

CABBAGE AND PEAS
Patta Gobi Mattar

INGREDIENTS

½ lb Cabbage (*bandh gobi*), cut into 1½" strips, rinsed, drained
¾ cup Green peas (*hara mattar*), shelled
1½ tbsp Vegetable oil
a pinch Asafetida (*hing*)
½ tsp Cumin (*jeera*) seeds
1 Green chili, slit
¼ tsp Turmeric (*haldi*) powder
Salt to taste
¼ tsp *Garam masala* (see p. 184)
2 tbsp Cilantro (*dhaniya*) leaves, chopped

METHOD

• Heat 1½ tbsp oil in a pan for 30 seconds; add asafetida, cumin seeds, green chili, and turmeric powder.

• Add green peas and cook for 30 seconds. Add cabbage and salt to taste; mix and cook covered on medium heat until soft.

• Add *garam masala* and cilantro leaves; mix and serve hot.

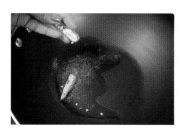

• This is a quick and healthy vegetable dish.
• Frozen peas can also be used.

GRAM FLOUR COATED ZUCCHINI
Besani Zucchini

INGREDIENTS

2 Zucchini, medium-sized, cut diagonally to 1" pieces
1½ tbsp Vegetable oil
¼ tsp Carom (*ajwain*) seeds
¼ tsp Cumin (*jeera*) seeds
1 tbsp Gram flour (*besan*)
¼ tsp Turmeric (*haldi*) powder
1 tsp Red chili powder
2 tsp Ground coriander (*dhaniya*)
Salt to taste
¼ tsp Mango powder (*amchur*)
½ tsp *Chaat masala*
2 tbsp Cilantro (*dhaniya*) leaves, chopped

METHOD

- Heat 1½ tbsp oil in a pan for 30 seconds; add carom seeds, cumin seeds, gram flour, and turmeric powder. Cook for 10 seconds.

- Add cut zucchini, red chili powder, cilantro, and salt to taste; cook for 2 minutes on high heat, stirring frequently.

- Add mango powder, *chaat masala*, and cilantro leaves; cook for a minute. Serve hot.

- Zucchini has a shiny outer skin that is edible.
- Yellow zucchini is also available.

- Zucchini, cut into fingers and served with any dressing, makes a good salad.

HEALTHY LEAFY VEGETABLE
Hara Saag

INGREDIENTS

1 lb *Hara saag*, hard threads from stalks removed, chopped into fine pieces, washed, drained
2 tbsp Mustard (*sarson*) oil / Vegetable oil
¼ tsp Fenugreek seeds (*methi dana*)
2 tsp Ginger (*adrak*), chopped
1 tsp Green chilies, chopped
2 Dry red chilies (*sookhi lal mirch*)
Salt to taste

METHOD

• Heat 2 tbsp oil in a pan for 30 seconds; add fenugreek seeds, ginger, green chilies, dry red chilies, and *saag*; mix well. Cook, covered, for 2 minutes on high heat.

• Uncover, add salt and cook open on high heat until the water evaporates, stirring occasionally. Serve hot.

• *Cholai* is a green leafy plant whose leaves and tender stems are cooked as *saag*. This *saag* is also available with a reddish tint.

• This *saag* is also called *cholai saag* or *dandi khere*.

CURRIED LOTUS STEMS
Sookhi Kamal Kakri

INGREDIENTS

½ lb Lotus stems (*kamal kakri*), peeled
3 tbsp Vegetable oil
2 Onions, medium-sized, peeled, grated
½ tsp Ginger (*adrak*) paste (see p. 191)
¾ tsp Red chili powder
½ tsp Turmeric (*haldi*) powder
4 Tomatoes, medium-sized, liquidized (see p. 187)
Salt to taste
2 tbsp Cilantro (*dhaniya*) leaves, chopped

METHOD

- Cut the lotus stems diagonally to ¼" pieces.

- Pressure cook the lotus stems with 2 cups water to one whistle and simmer for 2 minutes. Cool and drain.

- Heat 3 tbsp oil in a pan; add grated onion and fry until golden brown. Add ginger paste, red chili powder, and turmeric powder; mix well.

- Add liquidized tomato and cook until semi-thick. Add lotus stems and salt; cook, stirring occasionally, for 10 minutes or until dry.

- Serve hot garnished with cilantro leaves.

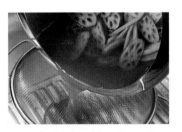

- While buying lotus stems, select the white ones with closed ends as the open-ended ones are muddy inside.
- Boiled lotus stem can also be used to prepare a spicy *chaat*.
- Lotus stem is considered a delicacy in Indian vegetarian cooking.

SWEET PUMPKIN
Meetha Kaddu

Serves: 4-6

INGREDIENTS

½ lb Red pumpkin (*kaddu*), peeled, cut into ¾" cubes. Cut the peels into 1" pieces.
2 tbsp Vegetable oil
a pinch Asafetida (*hing*)
½ tsp Fenugreek seeds (*methi dana*)
2 tsp Ginger (*adrak*), chopped
1 tsp Green chilies, chopped
½ tsp Turmeric (*haldi*) powder
½ tsp Red chili powder
Salt to taste
½ tsp Mango powder (*amchur*)
1 tbsp Jaggery (*gur*), powdered
2 tbsp Cilantro (*dhaniya*) leaves, chopped

METHOD

- Heat 2 tbsp oil in a pan for 30 seconds; add asafetida and fenugreek seeds; sauté until brown. Add ginger; green chilies, turmeric powder, red chili powder, and cut peels; cook for a minute. Add cut pumpkin and mix.

- Add salt to taste and ½ cup water; cook, covered, on high heat, stirring occasionally until the water evaporates.

- Uncover; add mango powder and jaggery; cook for a minute.

- Add cilantro leaves; mix well. Serve hot.

- *Meetha kaddu* is a festival dish and is accompanied with *aloo tamatar rasedar* (see p. 109) and *urad dal kachori* (see p. 140).

STUFFED BITTER GOURD
Bharwa Karela

INGREDIENTS

½ lb Bitter gourd (*karela*), peeled, slit vertically with a sharp knife, keeping shape intact
Salt to apply inside bitter gourd
2 tbsp Mustard oil / Vegetable oil
a pinch Asafetida (*hing*)
¼ Fenugreek seeds (*methi dana*)

For the stuffing: mix together
1½ tsp Ground fennel (*saunf*)
¾ tsp Ground coriander (*dhaniya*)
½ tsp Red chili powder
½ tsp Turmeric (*haldi*) powder
½ tsp Mango powder (*amchur*)
a pinch Asafetida
Salt to taste

METHOD

- Apply one pinch salt inside each bitter gourd and leave aside for half an hour. Wash and squeeze the water out.

- Fill each bitter gourd with the stuffing evenly. Set aside.

- Heat 1 tbsp mustard oil in a pressure cooker for 30 seconds; add asafetida, fenugreek seeds, and stuffed bitter gourd; mix. Add ¼ cup water and cook to one whistle, on high heat. Reduce and simmer for 3 minutes and cool.

- Transfer bitter gourd to a non-stick pan; cook until the water evaporates. Add 1 tbsp oil and cook for 10 minutes on low heat, turning occasionally, until light golden brown. Serve hot.

- Tender, small bitter gourd tastes better because it is seedless.

- *Bharwa karela* can be kept at room temperature for 4 days after cooking, hence it is a good traveling food item.

MIXED VEGETABLES WITH COTTAGE CHEESE
Sabz Paneer

INGREDIENTS

½ lb Cottage cheese (*paneer*), cut into 1" fingers (see p. 188)
8 Green beans, cut diagonally to 1" pieces
2 Carrots (*gajar*), medium-sized, cut diagonally to 1" pieces
1 Bell pepper (*Shimla mirch*), medium-sized, cut diagonally to 1" pieces
2 tbsp Vegetable oil
Salt to taste
¼ tsp Sugar
$1/_8$ tsp Turmeric (*haldi*) powder
½ tsp Red chili powder
2 Tomatoes, medium-sized, cut into cubes
1 tbsp Tomato sauce
¼ tsp *Garam masala* (see p. 184)

METHOD

- Heat 1 tbsp oil in a pan for 30 seconds; add cut green beans, carrots, bell pepper, sugar, and salt; cook, covered, on medium heat for 2 minutes. Remove and set aside.

- Heat 1 tbsp oil in the same pan; add turmeric powder, red chili powder, and cut tomatoes; cook for a minute.

- Add tomato sauce, cottage cheese, and salt to taste; cook, covered, for a minute. Add cooked vegetables and *garam masala*; mix well and cook for a minute. Serve hot.

- *Sabz paneer* can be served any time with any meal.
- *Sabz paneer* is a healthy combination of protein, calcium, and fiber.

TOMATO FLAVORED MIXED VEGETABLES
Milijuli Videshi Tarkariyan

INGREDIENTS

½ lb Broccoli, cut into 1½"
florets, blanched for a minute,
drained
¼ lb Mushrooms (*khumb*), cut
into half, blanched for 20
seconds, drained
¾ cup Red pepper, seeded, cut
into fingers
¾ cup Yellow pepper, seeded,
cut into fingers
1½ tbsp Vegetable oil
2 Onions, medium-sized,
chopped
1 tsp Garlic (*lasan*) paste
(see p. 191)
½ tsp Green chili paste
(see p. 191)
2 Tomatoes, medium-sized,
chopped
½ tsp *Chaat masala*
Salt to taste

For the tomato *masala*:
2 Tomatoes, medium-sized,
liquidized (see p. 187)
2 tsp Vegetable oil
¼ tsp Red chili powder
1 tsp Ground coriander
(*dhaniya*)
1 tbsp Tomato sauce
¼ tsp *Garam masala*
(see p. 184)
Salt to taste

METHOD

- **For the tomato *masala*,** heat
2 tsp oil in a pan for 30
seconds; add red chili powder,
cilantro powder, liquidized
tomato, tomato sauce, *garam
masala*, and salt; cook on
medium heat until the
mixture thickens. Set aside.

- Heat 1½ tbsp oil in a pan for
30 seconds; add the onions
and cook for a minute. Add
garlic and green chili pastes;
cook for 10 seconds.

- Add red and yellow pepper,
tomatoes, broccoli, and
mushrooms; cook for a
minute on high heat.

- Add the tomato *masala*,
chaat masala, and salt to
taste; cook on high heat
for a minute. Serve hot.

- Mixed vegetables taste best when mixed with tomato *masala* just
before serving.

HOT POTATO CURRY
Aloo ka Jhol

Serves: 4

INGREDIENTS
4 Potatoes, medium-sized,
boiled (see p. 183), peeled,
broken into small pieces
1 tbsp Vegetable oil
a pinch Asafetida (*hing*)
1 tsp Cumin (*jeera*) seeds
2 tsp Ginger (*adrak*), chopped
1 tsp Green chilies, chopped
½ tsp Turmeric (*haldi*) powder
½ tsp Red chili powder
Salt to taste
½ tsp Mango powder (*amchur*)
½ tsp *Garam masala*
(see p. 184)
2 tbsp Cilantro (*dhaniya*) leaves,
chopped

METHOD
- Heat 1 tbsp oil in a pan for
  30 seconds; add asafetida,
  cumin seeds, ginger, and green
  chilies; mix.

- Add turmeric powder, red
  chili powder, potatoes, and
  1½ cups water; mix well.

- Add salt to taste, mango
  powder, *garam masala*, and
  cilantro leaves; bring to a boil.
  Reduce heat and simmer for
  5 minutes. Serve hot.

- This potato dish is generally served with *meetha kaddu* (see p. 104), *sada paratha* (see p. 131), and *urad dal kachori* (see p. 140).

- Boiled potatoes are normally kept handy in Indian homes. They can be stored in the refrigerator for up to a week.

POTATOES IN TOMATO GRAVY
Aloo Tamatar Rasedar

Serves: 4-6

INGREDIENTS

4 Potatoes, medium-sized,
peeled, cut into 1" cubes,
immersed in water
3 Tomatoes, medium-sized,
liquidized (see p. 187)
1½ tbsp Vegetable oil
a pinch Asafetida (hing)
1 tsp Cumin (jeera) seeds
½ tsp Turmeric (haldi) powder
¾ tsp Red chili powder
1 tsp Ginger (adrak) paste
(see p. 191)
½ tsp Green chili paste
(see p. 191)
Salt to taste
2 tbsp Cilantro (dhaniya) leaves,
chopped
¼ tsp Garam masala
(see p. 184)

METHOD

- Heat 1½ tbsp oil in a pressure cooker for 30 seconds; add asafetida, cumin seeds, turmeric powder, red chili powder, ginger paste, and green chili paste; mix well. Add liquidized tomato and cook for 2 minutes.

- Add cut potatoes, 1¾ cups water, and salt. Pressure cook to one whistle, simmer for 5 minutes and turn off the heat, cool.

- Uncover the lid, add cilantro leaves and garam masala; bring to a boil, simmer for 2 minutes. Remove and serve hot.

- This dish can also be prepared with boiled potatoes and cooked in a pan instead of a pressure cooker.

- Chopped ginger and chopped chilies can also be liquidized along with the tomatoes.

CURRIED COLOCASIA
Rasedar Arvi

INGREDIENTS

½ lb Colocasia (*arvi*), peeled, cut into small fingers
Vegetable oil for cooking and deep-frying
2 Onions, medium-sized, grated
½ tsp Red chili powder
½ tsp Turmeric (*haldi*) powder
½ tsp Ground coriander (*dhaniya*)
½ cup Yogurt (*dahi*), 2-day-old, beaten (see p. 198)
Salt to taste
1 tbsp Cilantro (*dhaniya*) leaves, chopped
2 tsp Mint (*pudina*), chopped
¼ tsp *Garam masala* (see p. 184)

METHOD

- Heat 1"-deep oil in a shallow pan; deep-fry colocasia fingers in medium-hot oil to light golden brown. Set aside.

- Heat 2 tbsp oil in a pan for 30 seconds; add grated onion and fry until golden brown.

- Add red chili powder, turmeric powder, and ground coriander; mix.

- Add beaten yogurt and fry until oil separates.

- Add fried colocasia fingers, 1½ cups water, and salt to taste; bring to a boil and simmer for 5 minutes.

- Add cilantro leaves, mint, and *garam masala*; mix. Serve hot.

- Beat yogurt well, before adding to the gravy, to avoid separation.
- *Sada paratha* (see p. 131) is generally served with this dish.

CHICKPEAS WITH SPINACH GRAVY
Chana Palak

INGREDIENTS

1 cup Chickpeas (*kabuli chana*), soaked for 8 hours in plenty of water, drained
1 lb Spinach (*palak*), chopped, washed, drained in a colander
1 tbsp Vegetable oil
Salt to taste

Coarsely powdered:

½ tsp Cumin (*jeera*) seeds
2 Cloves (*laung*)
4 Black peppercorns (*sabut kali mirch*)

For the garnishing:

1 tbsp Vegetable oil
1 Onion, large, cut into medium-sized cubes
2 tsp Ginger (*adrak*), chopped
2 Tomatoes, medium-sized, cut into cubes
Salt to taste

METHOD

- Pressure cook soaked chickpeas with 1¼ cups water and ¼ tsp salt to one whistle, simmer for 20 minutes, cool. Drain.

- Heat a pan for 30 seconds; add spinach and cook covered for 2 minutes. Remove and cool. Grind coarsely in a food processor. Set aside.

- Heat 1 tbsp oil in a pan for 30 seconds; add coarsely powdered spices and cook for 10 seconds. Add boiled chickpeas and cook for a minute. Add puréed spinach and salt to taste; bring to a boil and simmer for 2 minutes. Transfer to a serving dish.

- **For the garnishing**, heat 1 tbsp oil in a pan; add onion and cook for a minute. Add ginger, tomatoes, and salt. Cook for 30 seconds. Pour this mixture evenly over the chickpeas. Serve hot.

- The same recipe can be used to make Corn and Spinach or Cottage Cheese and Spinach.
- Use 1 cup sweet corn for Corn and Spinach and ½ lb cottage cheese for Cottage Cheese and Spinach.

111 || MAIN COURSES || Pure & Simple

SPICY CHICKPEAS
Chana Masala

INGREDIENTS

1 cup Chickpeas (*kabuli chana*), soaked for 8 hours in plenty of water, drained
¼ tsp Baking soda
2 tbsp Vegetable oil
1 tsp Cumin (*jeera*) seeds
2 Onions, large, chopped into small pieces
1 tsp Garlic (*lasan*) paste (see p. 191)
1 tsp Red chili powder
2 tsp Ground coriander (*dhaniya*)
5 Tomatoes, medium-sized, liquidized (see p. 187)
2 Green chilies, slit
1 tbsp Ginger (*adrak*), julienned
2 tsp *Chana masala*
2 tbsp Pomegranate seed (*anar dana*) powder
Salt to taste
2 tbsp Cilantro (*dhaniya*) leaves, chopped

Coarsely ground:

4 Cloves (*laung*)
2 Black cardamom (*badi elaichi*)
2 Green cardamom (*choti elaichi*)
1" Cinnamon (*dalchini*) stick

METHOD

- Pressure cook chickpeas with baking soda and 2½ cups water (see p. 193).

- Heat 2 tbsp oil in a pan for 30 seconds; add cumin seeds, onions, and garlic paste; fry until light brown. Add coarsely powdered spices and mix.

- Add red chili powder, coriander, and liquidized tomato; fry until oil separates.

- Add boiled chickpeas along with water, green chilies, ginger, *chana masala*, pomegranate seed powder, and salt. Bring the mixture to a boil and simmer for 10 minutes.

- Add cilantro leaves. Serve hot.

- Pomegranate seed powder is available in any Indian grocery store. It is basically dried and powdered pomegranate seeds. The color of the dish changes to dark brown after adding this powder.

- This dish can be garnished with cut tomatoes, onions, ginger, and chilies.
- Spicy Chickpeas is a popular Indian dish that is usually accompanied with *bhatura* (see p. 141).

TANGY BOTTLE GOURD
Lauki Tamatardar

Serves: 4-6

INGREDIENTS

1 lb Bottle gourd (*lauki*), peeled, cut into 1" cubes
2 Tomatoes, medium-sized, grated (see p. 186)
1 tsp Clarified butter (*ghee*)
a pinch Asafetida (*hing*)
½ tsp Cumin (*jeera*) seeds
2 tsp Ginger (*adrak*), chopped
½ tsp Turmeric (*haldi*) powder
Salt to taste
2 tbsp Cilantro (*dhaniya*) leaves, chopped

METHOD

- Heat 1 tsp clarified butter in a pressure cooker for 30 seconds; add asafetida, cumin seeds, ginger, turmeric powder, and bottle gourd; mix well.

- Add 1 cup water and salt and pressure cook to one whistle. Reduce heat and simmer for 5 minutes. Cool.

- Uncover, add grated tomato and cook until semi-thick.

- Add cilantro leaves and mix. Serve hot.

- Bottle gourd is a light vegetable, generally recommended to those with digestive troubles and the calorie-conscious.
- This dish can also be prepared without tomatoes.

BOTTLE GOURD DUMPLINGS IN TOMATO GRAVY
Lauki Kofta

Serves: 4-6

INGREDIENTS

For the koftas:

½ lb Bottle gourd (*lauki*), peeled, grated

a pinch Asafetida (*hing*)

4 tbsp Gram flour (*besan*)

¼ tsp Salt

1 tbsp Cilantro (*dhaniya*) leaves, chopped

Vegetable oil for deep-frying

For the gravy:

1½ tbsp Vegetable oil

a pinch Asafetida

1 tsp Cumin (*jeera*) seeds

½ tsp Turmeric (*haldi*) powder

¾ tsp Red chili powder

1 tsp Ginger (*adrak*), chopped

4 Tomatoes, medium-sized, liquidized (see p. 187)

2 tbsp Yogurt (*dahi*), beaten (see p. 198)

Salt to taste

¼ tsp *Garam masala* (see p. 184)

1 tbsp Cilantro leaves, chopped

METHOD

- **For the koftas,** mix the grated bottle gourd with asafetida, gram flour, salt, and cilantro leaves. Divide the mixture equally into 20 balls.

- Heat 1"-deep oil in a shallow pan; deep-fry, 10 balls at a time, in medium-hot oil, until light golden brown. Set aside. Repeat until all are fried.

- **For the gravy,** heat 1½ tbsp oil in a pan for 30 seconds; add asafetida, cumin seeds, turmeric powder, red chili powder, and ginger; mix. Add liquidized tomato and fry until the oil separates. Add beaten yogurt and cook for a minute.

- Add the fried balls, 3 cups water, and salt. Bring the mixture to a boil reduce heat and simmer for 5 minutes. Add *garam masala* and cilantro leaves; mix well. Serve hot.

- Don't leave the bottle gourd mixed with gram flour and salt for a long time as it will become watery, making it difficult to shape into balls.

- Grated bottle gourd turns brown if left unused for a long time, so grate just before preparing.

LEMON FLAVORED RIDGE GOURD
Rasedar Turai

Serves: 4

INGREDIENTS

2 lb Ridge gourd (*turai*), peeled, cut into ½" semi-circles
1 tsp Clarified butter (*ghee*)
a pinch Asafetida (*hing*)
½ tsp Cumin (*jeera*) seeds
$\frac{1}{8}$ tsp Turmeric (*haldi*) powder
Salt to taste
2 tbsp Cilantro (*dhaniya*) leaves, chopped
½ tsp Lemon (*nimbu*) juice

METHOD

- Heat 1 tsp clarified butter in a pressure cooker for 30 seconds; add asafetida, cumin seeds, turmeric powder, ridge gourd, and salt; mix. Pressure cook to one whistle. Cool.

- Uncover pressure cooker lid and bring the mixture to a boil.

- Add cilantro leaves and lemon juice; mix well and turn off the heat. Serve hot.

- Ridge gourd can also be cooked in a pan on low heat until soft.
- Ridge gourd is easy to digest and served as a part of a light Indian meal.

BLACK-EYED PEAS IN GRAVY
Lobhia Taridar

Serves: 4-6

INGREDIENTS

1 cup Black-eyed peas (*lobhia*), soaked for 4 hours in plenty of water, drained
Salt to taste
½ tsp Turmeric (*haldi*) powder (¼ + ¼)
1 tbsp Vegetable oil
a pinch Asafetida (*hing*)
$\frac{1}{3}$ tsp Cumin (*jeera*) seeds
½ tsp Red chili powder
3 Tomatoes, medium-sized, liquidized (see p. 187)
1 tsp Ginger (*adrak*) paste (see p. 191)
¼ tsp Green chili paste (see p. 191)
Salt to taste
¼ tsp *Garam masala* (see p. 184)
2 tbsp Cilantro (*dhaniya*) leaves, chopped

METHOD

- Pressure cook the black-eyed peas with 2 cups water, salt, and ¼ tsp turmeric powder to one whistle; simmer for 5 minutes and cool (see p. 193).

- Heat 1 tbsp oil in a pan for 30 seconds; add asafetida, cumin seeds, red chili powder, ¼ tsp turmeric powder, liquidized tomato, ginger paste, and green chili paste; fry until oil separates. Add boiled black-eyed peas along with the water.

- Add salt to taste and bring to a boil. Reduce heat and simmer on low heat until semi-thick. Add *garam masala* and cilantro leaves. Serve hot.

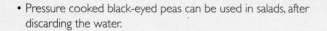

- Pressure cooked black-eyed peas can be used in salads, after discarding the water.

COTTAGE CHEESE WITH PEAS IN GRAVY
Mattar Paneer

Serves: 4-6

INGREDIENTS

½ lb Cottage cheese (*paneer*), cut into slices (see p. 188)

2 cups Green peas (*hara mattar*), boiled

4 tbsp Vegetable oil

2 Bay leaves (*tej patta*)

2 Onions, medium-sized, grated

1 tsp Ginger (*adrak*) paste (see p. 191)

¾ tsp Red chili powder

¾ tsp Turmeric (*haldi*) powder

3 Tomatoes, medium-sized, liquidized (see p. 187)

2 tbsp Yogurt (*dahi*), beaten (see p. 198)

2 tbsp Heavy cream

a pinch Sugar

¼ tsp *Garam masala* (see p. 184)

1 tbsp Cilantro (*dhaniya*) leaves, chopped

METHOD

- Heat 1 tbsp oil in a non-stick pan for 30 seconds; add cottage cheese and fry, on medium heat, on both sides until light brown (see p. 189). Remove, cool, and cut into 1" cubes. Set aside.

- Heat 3 tbsp oil in a pan for 30 seconds; add bay leaves, grated onion, and ginger paste; fry until light golden brown, stirring occasionally. Add red chili powder and turmeric powder; mix well. Add liquidized tomato and fry until the oil separates. Add beaten yogurt and fry until oil separates.

- Add cream, green peas, and cottage cheese; cook for a minute.

- Add 1½ cups water, salt to taste, and sugar. Bring to a boil and simmer for 5 minutes. Add *garam masala* and cilantro leaves; mix. Serve hot.

- Cream adds a better texture and taste to this gravy. Calorie watchers can avoid the cream.

- This onion-tomato gravy can be used for other gravy dishes as well.

LENTIL DUMPLINGS WITH FENUGREEK AND PEAS
Methi Magori Mattar

INGREDIENTS

1 cup Dry lentil dumplings (*magori*)

1½ cups Fenugreek (*methi*) leaves, chopped, cooked (see p. 196)

¾ cup Green peas (*hara mattar*), boiled

Vegetable oil for cooking and deep-frying

Salt to taste

a pinch Asafetida (*hing*)

½ tsp Cumin (*jeera*) seeds

½ tsp Ginger (*adrak*) paste (see p. 191)

¼ tsp Green chili paste (see p. 191)

½ tsp Red chili powder

½ tsp Turmeric (*haldi*) powder

3 Tomatoes, medium-sized, liquidized (see p. 187)

¼ tsp *Garam masala* (see p. 184)

2 tbsp Cilantro (*dhaniya*) leaves, chopped

METHOD

- Heat ½"-deep oil in a shallow pan; deep-fry the lentil dumplings in medium-hot oil until light golden (see p. 185) brown. Set aside.

- Heat 2 tsp oil in a pan for 30 seconds; add boiled peas and cook for a minute. Add salt. Set aside.

- Heat 2 tsp oil in a pressure cooker; add fried lentil dumplings, 2 cups water, and salt. Cook until one whistle, then simmer for 5 minutes, cool. Set aside.

- Heat 1 tbsp oil in a pan for 30 seconds; add asafetida, cumin seeds, ginger paste, green chili paste, red chili powder, and turmeric powder; mix. Add liquidized tomato and bring to a boil. Cook for 2 minutes, on medium heat. Add fenugreek leaves and cook for a minute.

- Add pressure cooked dumplings along with water and bring to a boil, simmer for 5 minutes. Add *garam masala* and mix.

- Add cooked peas and cilantro leaves; cook for 2 minutes. Serve hot.

- This dish is relished with *sada roti* (see p. 137).

- Fenugreek leaves add a delicate bitter flavor to the dish.

BITTER SWEET CREAMY PEAS
Methi Malai Mattar

INGREDIENTS

1 cup Green peas (*hara mattar*), boiled

1½ cups Fenugreek (*methi*) leaves, chopped

Salt to taste

1½ tbsp Vegetable oil

1 Onion, large, grated

1 tsp Ginger (*adrak*) paste (see p. 191).

½ tsp Garlic (*lasan*) paste (see p. 191)

½ tsp Red chili powder

½ tsp Ground coriander

2 Tomatoes, medium-sized, grated (see p. 186)

2 tsp Butter

1 tbsp Heavy cream

2 tbsp Milk

¼ tsp Sugar

¼ tsp *Garam masala* (see p. 184)

METHOD

- Add ½ tsp salt to fenugreek leaves, mix and leave aside for 5 minutes. Squeeze and set aside.

- Heat 1½ tbsp oil in a pan for 30 seconds, add grated onion, ginger and garlic pastes; cook on medium heat until light pink. Add squeezed fenugreek leaves and cook for a minute. Add red chili powder and coriander; mix well.

- Add grated tomato and cook for a minute.

- Add boiled peas, white butter, cream, milk, salt to taste, and sugar, bring to a boil and simmer for 2 minutes. Add *garam masala* and mix well. Serve hot.

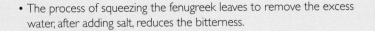

- The process of squeezing the fenugreek leaves to remove the excess water, after adding salt, reduces the bitterness.

RICE & BREADS

PEAS AND CARROT PILAF
Gajar Mattar Pulao

INGREDIENTS

1 cup Basmati rice
2 Carrots (*gajar*), medium-sized, chopped
½ cup Green peas (*hara mattar*)
1 tbsp Clarified butter (*ghee*)
2 Cloves (*laung*)
½ tsp Cumin (*jeera*) seeds
2 cups Water
Salt to taste

METHOD

- Wash and soak the rice in plenty of water for 20 minutes. Drain.

- Heat 1 tbsp clarified butter in a pan for 30 seconds; add cloves, cumin seeds, peas, and carrots. Cook for a minute on medium heat.

- Add soaked rice, 2 cups water, and salt to taste; bring to a boil and cook, covered, on low heat, till water evaporates or until rice is done. Serve hot.

- To get good textured rice, it is advised to cook it, covered, on low heat, after one boil.
- Stirring rice constantly while cooking breaks the grains.

- Any pilaf accompanied by flavored yogurt, of your choice, is a complete meal.

CORN PILAF
Bhutte ka Pulao

INGREDIENTS
1 cup Basmati rice
1 cup Corn (*bhutta*)
1 tbsp Clarified butter (*ghee*)
¼ tsp Black pepper (*kali mirch*)
1" Cinnamon (*dalchini*) stick
½ cup Scallions (*hara pyaz*), chopped
½ cup Green pepper (*Shimla mirch*), chopped
2 cups Water
Salt to taste

METHOD
- Wash and soak the rice in plenty of water for 30 minutes. Drain.

- Heat 1 tbsp clarified butter in a pan for 30 seconds: add black pepper and cinnamon stick.

- Add chopped scallions, pepper, and corn; cook for 30 seconds.

- Add soaked rice, 2 cups water, and salt to taste; bring to a boil. Cover and cook on low heat until water evaporates or until rice is done. Serve hot.

- The water quantity used to cook the rice should always be double the quantity of raw rice.

CUMIN PILAF
Jeera Pulao

INGREDIENTS

1 cup Basmati rice
1 tbsp Clarified butter (*ghee*)
2 Bay leaves (*tej patta*)
2 Black cardamom (*badi elaichi*)
4 Cloves (*laung*)
1" Cinnamon (*dalchini*) stick
1 tsp Cumin (*jeera*) seeds
2 cups Water
Salt to taste
1 tbsp Cilantro (*dhaniya*) leaves, chopped

METHOD

- Wash and soak the rice in plenty of water for 30 minutes. Drain.

- Heat 1 tbsp clarified butter in a pan for 30 seconds; add bay leaves, black cardamom, cloves, cinnamon stick, and cumin seeds; stir-fry.

- Add soaked rice and cook for 10 seconds.

- Add 2 cups water and salt to taste; bring to a boil. Cover and cook on low heat till the water evaporates or until rice is done.

- Serve hot garnished with cilantro leaves.

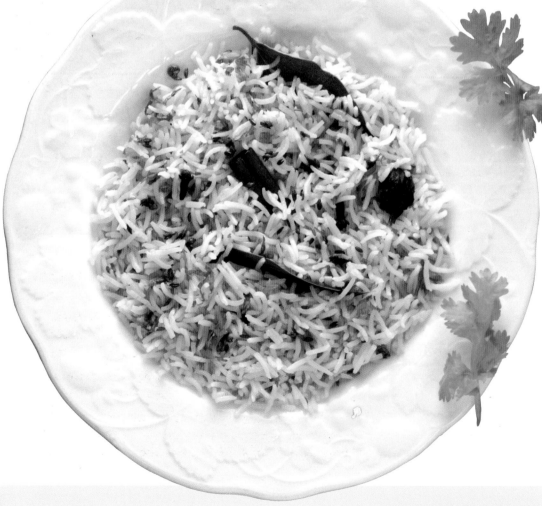

- Cumin pilaf is very safe to make as it goes with any combination of lentil and gravy dish.

- Basmati rice has a unique aroma and flavor, but any good quality long-grain rice can also be used.

MIXED VEGETABLE LENTIL RICE
Sabzion ki Kichadi

Serves: 2-4

INGREDIENTS
½ cup Rice, small grain
½ cup Split green gram (*dhuli moong dal*)
¾ cup Green peas (*hara mattar*)
¾ cup Carrots (*gajar*), chopped
¾ cup Cauliflower (*phool gobi*) florets
1 cup Potatoes, cubed
½ tsp Turmeric (*haldi*) powder
½ tsp Salt
2 tbsp Cilantro (*dhaniya*) leaves, chopped

For the tempering:
1 tbsp Clarified butter (*ghee*)
a pinch Asafetida (*hing*)
1 tsp Cumin (*jeera*) seeds
2 Cloves (*laung*)
2 Black cardamom (*badi elaichi*)
½" Cinnamon (*dalchini*) stick

METHOD
- Wash and soak the rice and green gram together in plenty of water for 30 minutes. Drain.

- Pressure cook the rice and green gram with cut vegetables, 3 cups water, salt, and turmeric powder to one whistle. Keep aside to cool.

- Uncover the pressure cooker lid and bring the mixture to a boil. Add cilantro leaves. Season with the tempering.

- **For the tempering,** heat 1 tbsp clarified butter in a pan for 30 seconds; add asafetida, cumin seeds, cloves, black cardamom, and cinnamon stick. Top it evenly over the rice mixture. Serve hot.

- *Kichadi* is always served with yogurt, pickle, and *papad*.
- *Kichadi* can also be prepared without vegetables.

- Use all forms of green gram except the whole (*sabut*) lentil.
- *Kichadi* is a complete one-dish meal.

FENUGREEK FLAVORED COTTAGE CHEESE PILAF
Methi Paneer Pulao

INGREDIENTS

1 cup Basmati rice
1 cup Fenugreek (*methi*) leaves, chopped
7 oz Cottage cheese (*paneer*), cut into slices (see p. 188)
2 tsp Vegetable oil
1½ tbsp Clarified butter (*ghee*)
2 Onions, medium-sized, cut into cubes
½ cup Cilantro (*dhaniya*) leaves, chopped
2 Tomatoes, medium-sized, cut into 8 pieces, liquidized (see p. 187)
2 cups Water
Salt to taste

METHOD

- Wash and soak the rice in plenty of water for 30 minutes. Drain.

- Heat 2 tsp oil in a non-stick pan for 30 seconds; sauté the cottage cheese till light golden brown on both sides. (see p. 189). Remove and cut into 1" cubes. Keep aside.

- Heat 1 tbsp clarified butter in a pan for 30 seconds; add chopped onions and fry till light brown. Add fenugreek leaves and cilantro leaves; cook for a minute.

- Add liquidized tomato and cook for a minute.

- Add soaked rice, 2 cups water, and salt to taste; bring to a boil. Cover and cook on low heat.

- When the rice is half-cooked, add cottage cheese and cook till the rice is done. Serve hot.

- *Pulao* is a rice dish containing spices to which vegetables may or may not be added.

MIXED VEGETABLE PILAF
Sabz Pulao

Serves: 2-4

INGREDIENTS
1 cup Basmati rice
2 Potatoes, medium-sized, cut into cubes
1 cup Cauliflower (*phool gobi*) florets
1 cup Green peas (*hara mattar*)
1 tbsp Clarified butter (*ghee*)
1 tsp Cumin (*jeera*) seeds
½ tsp Turmeric (*haldi*) powder
2 cups Water
1½ tsp Salt

METHOD
- Wash and soak the rice in plenty of water for 30 minutes. Drain.

- Heat 1 tbsp clarified butter in a pan for 30 seconds; add cumin seeds and turmeric powder. Add potatoes, cauliflower, and peas; mix well. Cook for a minute on medium heat. Add soaked rice and mix.

- Add 2 cups water and salt; bring to a boil. Cover and cook on low heat till the water evaporates or until rice is done.

- Soft firm texture of rice checked with index finger is considered to be done.
- Soaking helps the rice to cook properly and evenly.

- Always cook rice dishes in a flat pan to get better texture.
- This *pulao* is usually prepared in winter as peas and cauliflower are in abundance.

SPICY LENTIL RICE
Dal Biryani

INGREDIENTS

1 cup Basmati rice
¼ cup Yellow lentil (*arhar dal*)
Vegetable oil for deep-frying
2 Potatoes, medium-sized, cut into cubes
2 Onions, medium-sized, cut into flakes
1 tbsp Clarified butter (*ghee*)
2 cups Water
Salt to taste
¼ tsp *Garam masala* (see p. 184)
1 tbsp Cilantro (*dhaniya*) leaves, chopped

For seasoning 1:
½ tsp Cumin (*jeera*) seeds
½ tsp Ginger (*adrak*) paste (see p. 191)
½ tsp Garlic (*lasan*) paste (see p. 191)
½ tsp Green chili paste (see p. 191)

For seasoning 2:
½" Cinnamon (*dalchini*) stick
2 Black cardamom (*badi elaichi*)
¼ tsp Turmeric (*haldi*) powder

METHOD

• Wash and soak the rice and yellow lentil separately in plenty of water for 30 minutes. Drain.

• Deep-fry the potatoes in medium-hot oil till light golden brown. Remove and keep aside.

• Deep-fry the onions in hot oil till light golden brown. Remove and keep aside.

• Heat 1 tbsp clarified butter in a pan for 30 seconds; add all the ingredients of seasoning 1 and mix well. Add seasoning 2 and mix.

• Add soaked rice and lentil; cook for 30 seconds. Add 2 cups water and salt to taste; bring the mixture to a boil. Cover and cook on low heat, till water evaporates or until rice is done.

• Add fried potatoes and onions, and *garam masala*; mix. Serve hot garnished with cilantro leaves.

• This dish is a complete meal in itself with a combination of rice and lentil together.
• *Dal Biryani* can also be accompanied with plain yogurt.

TOMATO RICE
Tamatar ke Chawal

INGREDIENTS

1 cup Basmati rice
4 Tomatoes, medium-sized, cut into 8 pieces, liquidized (see p. 187)
1 tbsp Clarified butter (*ghee*)
¼ tsp Mustard seeds (*rai*)
¼ tsp Cumin (*jeera*) seeds
15 Curry leaves (*kadhi patta*)
2 tsp Bengal gram (*chana dal*), dehusked, split
2 tsp Black gram (*dhuli urad dal*), dehusked, split
2 Onions, medium-sized, chopped into medium-sized cubes
¼ tsp Turmeric (*haldi*) powder
¼ Red chili powder
Salt to taste
2 tbsp Cilantro (*dhaniya*) leaves, chopped
2 tbsp Peanuts (*moongphalli*), skinned

METHOD

- Wash and soak the rice in plenty of water for 30 minutes. Drain. Boil the rice (see p. 190) in water. Drain and keep aside.

- Heat 1 tbsp clarified butter in a pan for 30 seconds; add mustard seeds, cumin seeds, curry leaves, Bengal gram, and black gram; cook till light pink in color.

- Add the onions and cook till light brown. Add turmeric and red chili powders; mix. Add liquidized tomato and cook till thick.

- Add boiled rice and mix lightly.

- Add salt to taste, cilantro leaves, and peanuts; cook on low heat for 5 minutes, stirring occasionally. Serve hot.

- Leftover rice can also be used to prepare this dish.

- Tomato rice has a nutty flavor.

HEALTHY VEGETABLE PILAF
Hariyali Pulao

Serves: 4-6

INGREDIENTS

1 cup Basmati Rice
1 cup Broccoli florets
1½ cups Zucchini, cut diagonally
1½ cups Spinach (*palak*), chopped
1 tbsp Clarified butter (*ghee*)
¼ tsp Black pepper (*kali mirch*)
2 cups Water
Salt to taste

METHOD

- Wash and soak the rice in plenty of water for 20 minutes. Drain.

- Heat 1 tbsp clarified butter in a pan for 30 seconds, add black pepper and spinach, cook for 30 seconds. Add broccoli and zucchini, and cook for 30 seconds more.

- Add soaked rice, 2 cups water, and salt to taste; bring to a boil. Cook, covered, on low heat till done. Serve hot.

- *Hariyali pulao* is enjoyed by everyone because of its delicate flavoring and the natural taste of vegetables.

SHALLOW FRIED PLAIN BREAD
Sada Paratha

INGREDIENTS

2 cups Whole-wheat flour (*atta*)
½ tsp Salt
¾ cup Water to make the dough
Vegetable oil for shallow-frying

METHOD

- Sieve the whole-wheat flour with salt. Knead to make a normal dough with water (see p. 190). Keep covered for 10 minutes.

- Divide the dough into 12 equal balls. Take a ball, dust and roll with a rolling pin slightly, apply ½ tsp oil, sprinkle whole-wheat flour and fold into a triangle. Dust and roll into 5½" triangle.

- Shallow-fry each *paratha* on a heated griddle (*tawa*) with 2 tsp oil until light golden brown on both sides. Serve hot.

- Fold the *paratha* first into a semi-circle and then fold the semi-circle into a triangle.
- Fresh *paratha* can be fried soft or crisp as per individual taste.

- For storing *paratha*, fry lightly so that it remains soft.

INDIAN BREAD STUFFED WITH POTATOES
Aloo Paratha

INGREDIENTS

2 cups Whole-wheat flour (*atta*)
½ tsp Salt
½ tbsp Clarified butter (*ghee*), melted
¾ cup Water to prepare dough
Vegetable oil for shallow-frying

For the filling:

4 Potatoes, medium-sized, boiled (see p. 183), peeled, mashed
1 tsp Fennel (*saunf*) powder
1 tsp Green chilies, chopped
1 tbsp Cilantro (*dhaniya*) leaves, chopped
¼ tsp Mango powder (*amchur*)
Salt to taste

METHOD

• Sieve the whole-wheat flour with salt. Add clarified butter and knead to make a normal dough with water. Keep covered for 10 minutes.

• **For the filling,** mix the mashed potato with ground fennel, green chilies, cilantro leaves, mango powder, and salt to taste. Keep aside.

• Divide the dough and the filling each into 8 portions. Roll a portion of the dough slightly, stuff with 1 tbsp filling and fold to seal the filling inside. Dust with flour and roll with a rolling pin into a 6" disc.

• Add ½ tsp oil on a heated griddle (*tawa*) and shallow-fry each disc with 2 tbsp oil until light golden brown on both sides. Serve hot.

• Stuffed *paratha* is a quick and popular meal.
• Variations can be made by changing the base of the filling to grated cauliflower, grated cottage cheese, or chopped onions.
• It can be served with yogurt, pickle, and butter.
• For calorie watchers reduce oil while shallow-frying and omit butter while serving.

DOUBLE-DECKER INDIAN BREAD
Tiranga Paratha

INGREDIENTS

2 cups Whole-wheat flour (*atta*)

½ tsp Salt

1 tbsp Clarified butter (*ghee*), melted

¾ cup Water to make the dough

Vegetable oil for cooking

For filling 1:

7 oz Cottage cheese (*paneer*), grated (see p. 188)

½ tsp Black pepper (*kali mirch*)

2 tbsp Cilantro (*dhaniya*) leaves, chopped

Salt to taste

For filling 2:

½ tsp Green chili paste (see p. 191)

1 cup Green peas (*hara mattar*), boiled, mashed coarsely

1 tbsp Vegetable oil

½ tsp Mango powder (*amchur*)

¼ tsp *Garam masala* (see p. 184)

¼ tsp Salt

2 tbsp Cilantro leaves, chopped

METHOD

- Sieve the whole-wheat flour with salt. Add melted clarified butter and knead to make a normal dough (see p. 190) with water. Keep covered for 15 minutes.

- **For filling 1**, mix the grated cottage cheese with black pepper, cilantro leaves, and salt to taste. Keep aside.

- **For filling 2**, heat 1 tbsp oil in a pan for 30 seconds; add green chili paste and peas, cook for a minute. Add mango powder, *garam masala*, salt to taste, and cilantro leaves; cook on low heat for 2 minutes, stirring occasionally. Remove and set aside.

- Divide the dough into 21 balls.

- Take three balls, roll them slightly and place a portion of filling 1 on one round, cover with the second round and place a portion of filling 2 on the second round and cover with the third round.

- Press the edges, dust with flour and roll into a 7" disc. Shallow-fry each disc on a heated griddle (*tawa*) with 2 tbsp oil until light golden brown. Remove and serve hot.

- Approximately ¾ cup water is required to make the dough.
- *Tiranga paratha* can be served with plain yogurt or *raita*.
- *Tiranga paratha* makes an ideal Sunday breakfast.

FLAKY MINT BREAD
Lachchedar Paratha

INGREDIENTS

1 cup Whole-wheat flour (*atta*)
1 cup All-purpose flour (*maida*)
½ tsp Salt
½ cup Milk
¼ cup Water (approx.) to make the dough
Clarified butter (*ghee*) and Mint (*pudina*) powder (see p. 11) to apply inside
Vegetable oil / Clarified butter for cooking

METHOD

- Sieve both the flours with salt. Add milk and knead to make a soft dough with water. Keep covered for 15 minutes.

- Divide the dough equally into 5 balls; flatten each ball with a rolling pin, apply 2 tsp clarified butter, sprinkle ¼ tsp mint powder, and ½ tsp whole-wheat flour. Fold one end to another forming 1" pleats like a cylinder.

- Fold the cylinder to form a flat ball (*peda*). Dust and roll with a rolling pin into a 6" disc.

- Shallow-fry each *paratha* on a heated griddle (*tawa*) with 2 tbsp oil till light golden brown.

- Remove and crush along with a napkin. Serve hot.

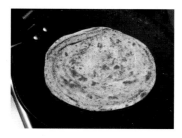

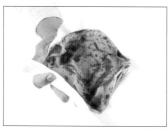

- Making a soft dough and sprinkling whole-wheat flour helps the layers to open easily.

- *Lachchedar paratha* can also be roasted directly on heat like *sada roti* (see p. 137).

CALABASH BREAD
Lauki Paratha

INGREDIENTS

1½ cups Whole-wheat flour (*atta*)
½ cup Gram flour (*besan*)
¾ tsp Salt
2 tbsp Yogurt (*dahi*)
½ lb Bottle gourd (*lauki*), grated
½ tsp Carom (*ajwain*) seeds
2 tbsp Cilantro (*dhaniya*) leaves, chopped
½ tsp Red chili powder
¼ tsp Turmeric (*haldi*) powder
Vegetable oil for cooking

METHOD

• Sieve the whole-wheat flour and gram flour with salt. Add yogurt, grated bottle gourd, carom seeds, cilantro leaves, red chili powder, and turmeric powder.

• Knead to make a normal dough (see p. 190) with water. Cover and set aside for 5 minutes.

• Divide the dough into 12 equal balls. Dust and roll each ball slightly with a rolling pin, apply ¼ tsp oil and fold into a triangle (see p. 131).

• Dust and roll again to 4" triangle.

• Shallow-fry each *paratha* on a heated griddle (*tawa*) with 1 tbsp oil until light golden brown. Serve hot.

• Bottle gourd leaves water if left unused for a long time. Always prepare fresh dough as it is easier to roll.

SPICY INDIAN BREAD
Masala Paratha

INGREDIENTS

2 cups Whole-wheat flour
(*atta*)
½ tsp Salt
2 tbsp Yogurt (*dahi*)
¾ cup Water to make the
dough
Vegetable oil for applying inside
and for shallow-frying
4 tbsp Cilantro (*dhaniya*) leaves,
chopped

**For the masala to apply inside:
mix together**

¼ tsp Asafetida (*hing*)
¾ tsp Salt
2 tsp Red chili powder
½ tsp Carom (*ajwain*) seeds
1 tsp Cumin (*jeera*) seeds

METHOD

- Sieve whole-wheat flour with salt. Add yogurt and knead to make a normal dough with water. Keep covered for 10 minutes.

- Divide the dough into 8 equal balls, dust each ball and roll into 6" diameter. Apply 2 tsp oil, sprinkle mixed *masala*, and cilantro leaves and cut into 12 pieces with a knife.

- Place each piece on top of the other covering the last piece from masala side down, press.

- Dust and roll again with a rolling pin to 6" diameter.

- Shallow-fry each *paratha* on a heated griddle (*tawa*) with 2 tbsp oil till light golden brown on both sides. Crush with palm. Serve hot.

- *Masala paratha* served with yogurt and pickle makes a sumptuous mini meal.

- *Masala paratha* is also called 16-layered *paratha* because the dough is cut into 16 pieces before rolling for the second time.

PLAIN INDIAN BREAD
Sada Roti

Serves: 4-6

INGREDIENTS

2 cups Whole-wheat flour (*atta*)
½ tsp Salt
¾ cup Water to make the dough
Clarified butter (*ghee*) for applying

METHOD

- Sieve whole-wheat flour with salt and knead to make a normal dough with water. Keep covered for 15 minutes.

- Divide the dough equally into 12-15 balls, dust with wheat flour and roll with a rolling pin into 4" discs.

- Place on a heated griddle (*tawa*) and cook on both sides.

- Remove and roast over the flame directly till light golden brown.

- Apply ½ tsp clarified butter with a spoon and serve hot.

- Roasting can also be done on the griddle with the help of a napkin.
- Calorie watchers can omit applying clarified butter.

FENUGREEK BREAD
Besan Methi Roti

INGREDIENTS

1 cup Gram flour (*besan*)
½ cup Whole-wheat flour (*atta*)
¼ tsp Baking soda
¾ tsp Salt
½ tsp Red chili powder
½ tsp Carom (*ajwain*) seeds
a pinch Asafetida (*hing*)
2 tbsp Yogurt (*dahi*)
1 cup Fenugreek (*methi*) leaves, chopped
Clarified butter (*ghee*) for applying

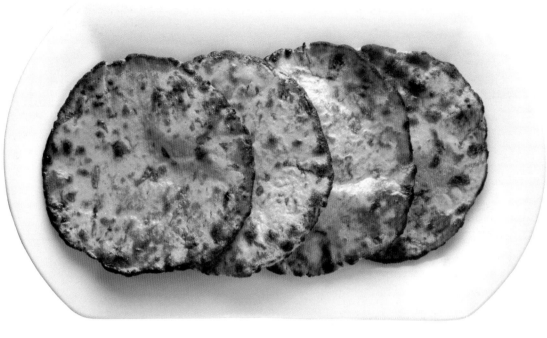

METHOD

- Sieve gram flour and whole-wheat flour with baking soda and salt. Add red chili powder, carom seeds, Asafetida, yogurt, and fenugreek leaves; mix and prepare a semi-hard dough (see p. 190) with water. Keep covered for 30 minutes.

- Divide the dough equally into 12 balls, dust each with wheat flour and roll with a rolling pin into 2½" disc.

- Place the disc on a heated griddle (*tawa*) and cook on both sides. Remove and roast over the flame directly until light brown.

- Apply ½ tsp clarified butter on each bread and serve hot.

- Gram flour consumes less water, hence it gets difficult to handle if the dough is too soft.

- This bread made with whole-wheat flour, gram flour, and fenugreek leaves has an unusual taste. It can be served for both lunch and dinner.

CRISP INDIAN BREAD
Khasta Roti

Serves: 2-4

INGREDIENTS

2 cups Whole-wheat flour (*atta*)
1 tsp Salt
1 tbsp Clarified butter (*ghee*),
melted
¾ cup Water to knead the
dough
Carom (*ajwain*) seeds to
sprinkle inside
Clarified butter for applying
inside and outside

METHOD

• Sieve the whole-wheat flour with salt. Add melted clarified butter and knead to make a semi-hard dough with water. Keep covered for 10 minutes.

• Divide the dough equally into 5 balls. Flatten each ball with a rolling pin, apply 1½ tsp clarified butter, sprinkle ¼ tsp carom seeds, and ¼ tsp whole-wheat flour evenly.

• Fold from one end of the disc to another like a cylinder. Press the cylinder with the palm to form a string and fold the string like a flat ball (*peda*). Dust and roll with a rolling pin into a 6" disc. Repeat with the others.

• Place the disc on a heated griddle (*tawa*), turn after 30 seconds and prick with a fork evenly. Roast over medium flame until light golden brown. Remove, apply 1 tsp clarified butter on top and serve hot.

• *Khasta roti* goes well with any variety of lentil.
• This *roti* looks flat but it is actually very crisp to taste.

LENTIL PUFFS
Urad Dal Kachori

INGREDIENTS

2 cups Whole-wheat flour (*atta*)
½ tsp Salt
Water to make the dough
Vegetable oil for deep-frying

For the filling:
1 cup Black gram (*dhuli urad dal*), de-husked, split
¼ tsp Asafetida (*hing*)
½ tsp Salt
1 tsp Red chili powder
2 tsp Fennel (*saunf*) powder
1 Potato, medium-sized, boiled, grated

METHOD

- Sieve the whole-wheat flour with salt and knead to make a normal dough (see p. 190) with water. Keep covered for 15 minutes.

- **For the filling**, wipe the black gram with a napkin and grind to a fine powder. Mix with Asafetida, salt, red chili powder, fennel powder, and ½ cup water. Keep covered for 30 minutes. Add potato, mix well and set aside.

- Divide the dough and filling each into 20 portions. Flatten the portion of the dough slightly, place 1 tsp filling and fold to seal the filling inside.

- Dust with flour and roll with a rolling pin into 3½" discs.

- Heat 1"-deep oil in a pan; fry the discs in hot oil until they puff out and become light golden brown. Serve hot.

- *Urad dal kachori*, served with *aloo ka jhol* (see p. 108) and *meetha kaddu* (see p. 104), is usually prepared on festivals like Holi and Diwali.

- Black gram consumes a lot of water. After adding water to black gram paste, it may look watery initially, but will become thick after 30 minutes.

THICK FLOUR PUFFS
Bhatura

Serves : 4-6

INGREDIENTS

2 cups All-purpose flour (*maida*)
$\frac{1}{3}$ cup Semolina (*suji*)
¼ tsp Baking soda
½ tsp Salt
½ tsp Baking powder
2 tbsp Yogurt (*dahi*), sour
1 tsp Sugar
Water to make the dough
Vegetable oil for deep-frying

METHOD

- Sieve the flour and semolina with baking soda, salt, and baking powder.

- Whisk yogurt with sugar and add to the flour mixture. Mix and knead to make a soft dough with water. Keep covered for 3 hours with a moist napkin.

- Divide the dough equally into 15 portions, lightly dust with flour and roll into oblong shape to 5-6" diameter.

- Heat 1"-deep oil in a pan; fry the puff in hot oil till light golden brown. Serve hot.

- All-purpose flour has an elastic texture and shrinks if not dusted with flour.
- *Bhatura* is served with *masala chana* (see p. 112), and is also accompanied with cut onions, pickle, and green chilies.
- Deep-fry the *bhatura* in hot oil otherwise they tend to consume more oil.

CAROM SPICED PUFFS
Namak Ajwain ki Puri

Serves: 4

INGREDIENTS
2 cups Whole-wheat flour (*atta*)
¾ tsp Salt
1 tsp Carom (*ajwain*) seeds
2 tsp Clarified butter (*ghee*), melted
Vegetable oil for deep-frying

METHOD
- Sieve whole-wheat flour with salt. Add carom seeds and melted clarified butter; knead to make a hard dough with water. Keep covered for 15 minutes.

- Divide the dough equally into 18 balls. Roll each ball out with a rolling pin to 3½" diameter.

- Heat 1"-deep oil in a shallow pan; deep-fry the discs in hot oil until light golden brown. Serve hot.

- *Namak ajwain ki puri* tastes best with *jeera aloo* (see p. 87), and *aam ka kas* (see p. 165).

SPICY ROASTED INDIAN BREAD
Aloo Kulcha

INGREDIENTS

2 cups All-purpose flour (*maida*)
½ tsp Salt
¼ tsp Baking soda
½ tsp Baking powder
2 tbsp Yogurt (*dahi*)
2 tbsp Milk
½ tsp Sugar
2 tbsp Vegetable oil
Water to make the dough
Butter for applying

For the filling: mix together

2 Potatoes, medium-sized, boiled, peeled, mashed
½ tsp Red chili powder
¼ tsp Mango powder (*amchur*)
¾ tsp Ground fennel (*saunf*)
¼ tsp Salt
2 tbsp Cilantro (*dhaniya*) leaves, chopped

For the topping:

2 tbsp Onion seeds (*kalonji*)= black caraway seeds
2 tbsp Cilantro leaves, chopped

METHOD

- Sieve the flour with salt, baking soda, and baking powder.

- Whisk the yogurt with milk and sugar; add to the dough along with oil and knead to make an extra soft dough with water. Keep covered for 2 hours.

- Divide the dough equally into 12 balls, flatten slightly, fill with 1 tsp filling and fold to seal the filling inside.

- Sprinkle caraway seeds and cilantro leaves on a flat surface, press each ball over it. Dust and roll with a rolling pin into 4" disc.

- Heat the gas tandoor or pressure cooker and stick the *kulcha* with the help of water on the back side and cook till light golden brown. Remove, apply butter and serve hot. Alternately, you can bake in the oven at 400°F for 4-6 minutes or until light brown.

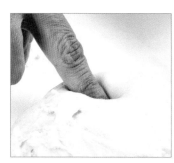

- *Aloo kulcha* can be served with any kind of lentil or vegetable.
- A soft dough gives a good texture to the *kulcha*.
- Do not apply water on the onion seeds and cilantro leaves side as this is the top side of the *kulcha*.

- *Kulcha* can be eaten with or without butter.
- This bread can also be made in a flat pan like a normal stuffed *roti*.

ACCOMPANIMENTS

POTATOES IN YOGURT
Aloo Raita

Serves: 4

INGREDIENTS

¾ cup Potatoes, boiled
(see p. 183), chopped
2 cups Yogurt (*dahi*), whisked
¼ cup Milk, chilled
Salt to taste
¼ tsp Ginger (*adrak*) paste
(see p. 191)
¼ tsp Green chili paste
(see p. 191)
¼ tsp Coriander (*dhaniya*) paste
¼ tsp Black salt (*kala namak*)

For the garnishing:

½ tsp Roasted cumin (*jeera*)
powder (see p. 184)
¼ tsp Red chili powder
1 tbsp Cilantro leaves, chopped

METHOD

- Whisk the yogurt and mix chilled milk, salt to taste, ginger paste, green chili paste, cilantro paste, and black salt.

- Add potatoes and mix.

- Serve chilled garnished with roasted ground cumin, red chili powder, and cilantro leaves.

- Always use chilled yogurt.
- Adding ¼ cup chilled milk checks the sourness of yogurt.

FRUITY YOGURT
Anar aur Ananas Raita

INGREDIENTS
¼ cup Pomegranate seeds
(*anar dana*)
¾ cup Pineapple (*ananas*)
pieces, canned or fresh
2 cups Yogurt (*dahi*), whisked
¼ cup Milk, chilled
Salt to taste
¼ tsp Confectioner's sugar
¼ tsp Mint (*pudina*) powder
(see p. 11) Or
½ tsp / Mint paste
¼ tsp Black pepper (*kali mirch*)
For the garnishing:
¼ tsp Roasted cumin (*jeera*)
powder (see p. 184)
1 tbsp Cilantro (*dhaniya*) leaves,
chopped

METHOD
- Whisk the yogurt and mix chilled milk, salt to taste, sugar, mint powder or paste, and black pepper.

- Add pineapple and pomegranate seeds; mix.

- Serve chilled garnished with roasted cumin powder and cilantro leaves.

- Any yogurt preparation, without cooking, mixed with herbs, fruits or vegetables, seasoned with salt, and served chilled is called *raita*.

- *Raita* has a cooling effect, hence is a good accompaniment to balance a spicy dish.

YOGURT WITH LENTIL PEARLS
Boondi Raita

Serves: 4

INGREDIENTS
¾ cup Gram flour pearls
(*boondi*)
2 cups Yogurt (*dahi*), whisked
¼ cup Milk, chilled
Salt to taste

For the garnishing:
½ tsp Roasted cumin (*jeera*)
powder (see p. 184)
¼ tsp Red chili powder
1 tbsp Cilantro (*dhaniya*) leaves,
chopped

METHOD
- Whisk yogurt with chilled milk, salt to taste, and gram flour pearls.

- Serve chilled garnished with roasted cumin powder, red chili powder, and cilantro leaves.

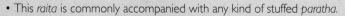

- This *raita* is commonly accompanied with any kind of stuffed *paratha*.
- *Boondi* can be soaked in 2½ cups water for half an hour, squeezed and then used. This helps to remove excess oil.
- *Boondi* packets are readily available in grocery stores.
- To prepare *boondi* at home see p. 168.

LENTIL DUMPLINGS IN CREAMY YOGURT
Dahi Pakodi

Serves: 4

INGREDIENTS

¾ cup Green gram (*moong dal*), washed, soaked in plenty of water for 3 hours, drained
1½ tbsp Black gram (*urad dal*), washed, soaked in plenty of water for 3 hours, drained
5 cups / 1 lt Yogurt (*dahi*), hung (see p. 198)
½-1 cup Milk, chilled
Salt to taste
Vegetable oil for deep-frying
Red chili powder to taste
Roasted cumin (*jeera*) powder (see p. 184) to taste
Cilantro (*dhaniya*) leaves, chopped for garnishing

METHOD

• Place the yogurt in a fine strainer for 2 hours, discard the water, remove from strainer and whisk. Add chilled milk to get a medium-thick consistency. Add salt to taste and refrigerate.

• Grind the lentils together with minimum water to get a thick consistency. Beat the mixture until light and fluffy.

• Heat 1"-deep oil in a shallow pan; drop small portions of batter with your fingers, a few at a time, and deep-fry in hot oil to light golden brown.

• Immerse the balls in 5 cups salted water for an hour. Squeeze within the palm to remove excess water, keep aside and refrigerate.

• Place squeezed balls in a serving dish and cover with yogurt mixture. Sprinkle red chili powder, cumin powder, and cilantro leaves and serve chilled. It is served along with sweet chutney (see p. 157) and green chutney (see p.154).

• Slightly coarse ground lentil gives a better texture to *dahi pakodi*.
• For salted water, mix 1 tsp salt into 5 cups water.

• *Dahi pakodi* is an integral part of a formal family meal in North India. It is served chilled.

YOGURT WITH GRATED BOTTLE GOURD
Lauki Raita

INGREDIENTS

½ lb Bottle gourd (*lauki*),
peeled, grated
2 cups Yogurt (*dahi*)
¼ cup Milk, chilled
Salt to taste

For the garnishing:
½ tsp Roasted cumin (*jeera*)
powder (see p. 184)
¼ tsp Red chili powder
1 tbsp Cilantro (*dhaniya*) leaves,
chopped

METHOD

- Pressure cook grated bottle
  gourd with 2 cups water to
  one whistle. Cool, drain, and
  squeeze.

- Whisk yogurt, add chilled milk,
  salt to taste, and squeezed
  bottle gourd; mix.

- Serve chilled garnished with
  roasted cumin powder, red
  chili powder, and cilantro
  leaves.

- For variation, grated and cooked red pumpkin can be used instead of
  bottle gourd.

LIQUID YOGURT SALAD
Kachumar Raita

INGREDIENTS

½ cup Cucumber (*khira*), chopped
¼ cup Onion, chopped
¼ cup Tomatoes, chopped
2 cups Yogurt (*dahi*)
¼ cup Milk, chilled
½ tsp Green chili paste (see p. 191)
Salt to taste

For the garnishing:

½ tsp Roasted cumin (*jeera*) powder (see p. 184)
1 tbsp Cilantro (*dhaniya*) leaves, chopped

METHOD

- Whisk yogurt, add chilled milk, green chili paste, and salt to taste; mix.

- Add cucumber, onion, and tomatoes; mix.

- Serve chilled garnished with roasted cumin powder and cilantro leaves.

- This *raita* can be served with any meal but it is a must with *dal biryani* (see p. 128).

TEMPERED LIQUID YOGURT
Tarka Mattha

INGREDIENTS

2½ cups Yogurt (*dahi*)
¾ cup Water
Salt to taste
¼ tsp Ginger (*adrak*) paste
(see p. 191)
¼ tsp Green chili paste
(see p. 191)
1 tsp Coriander (*dhaniya*) paste

For the tempering:
2 tsp Vegetable oil
a pinch Asafetida (*hing*)
¼ tsp Mustard seeds (*rai*)
2 Dry red chilies
(*sookhi lal mirch*)
6 Curry leaves (*kadhi patta*)

METHOD

• Whisk yogurt and add ¾ cup water.

• Add salt to taste, ginger paste, green chili paste, and coriander paste; mix well.

• **For the tempering**, heat 2 tsp oil in a pan for 30 seconds; add Asafetida, mustard seeds, dry red chilies, and curry leaves.

• Pour over the yogurt mixture and serve chilled.

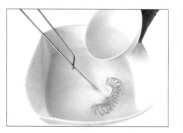

• Slightly sour yogurt is preferred for better taste.

• Such accompaniments make a meal interesting.

SPINACH FLAVORED YOGURT
Palak Raita

INGREDIENTS

1½ cups Spinach (*palak*), chopped
2 cups Yogurt (*dahi*)
¼ cup Milk, chilled
Salt to taste

For the tempering:
¼ tsp Clarified butter (*ghee*)
a pinch Asafetida (*hing*)
½ tsp Cumin (*jeera*) seeds
2 Dry red chilies (*sookhi lal mirch*)

METHOD

• Heat the pan for 30 seconds; add chopped spinach and cook covered for a minute (see p. 196). Remove and cool. Pound spinach to make a paste.

• Whisk yogurt and add milk, salt to taste, and spinach paste; mix.

• **For the tempering,** heat ¼ tsp clarified butter in a pan; add Asafetida, cumin seeds, and dry red chilies. Pour over the yogurt and serve chilled.

• For variation, use 2 tsp mint paste instead of spinach to make mint *raita*. Mint needs no cooking.

GREEN CHUTNEY
Hari Chutney

INGREDIENTS

2 cups Cilantro (*dhaniya*) leaves,
washed, drained in a colander
2 tsp Green chilies, chopped
½ tsp Cumin (*jeera*) seeds
a pinch Asafetida (*hing*)
½ tsp Ground coriander
(dhaniya)
1 tsp Salt
Lemon (*nimbu*) juice to taste

METHOD

- Grind cilantro leaves, green chilies, cumin seeds, Asafetida, ground coriander, and salt with minimum water to make a smooth paste.

- Transfer into a bowl.

- Add lemon juice just before serving.

- Lemon juice added to the chutney, just before serving, gives a fresh green color, but it fades after sometime because of the alkaline reaction of lemon.

CHERRY TOMATO CHUTNEY
Chhote Tamatar ki Chutney

INGREDIENTS

½ lb Cherry tomatoes, make a cross on each
2 tsp Vegetable oil
a pinch Asafetida (*hing*)
2 tsp Ginger (*adrak*), chopped
1 Green chili, slit
1 tbsp Raisins (*kishmish*)
Salt to taste
1½ tsp Sugar
¼ tsp Black pepper (*kali mirch*)
½ tsp Roasted cumin (*jeera*) powder (see p. 184)
1 tbsp Mint (*pudina*), chopped

METHOD

• Boil 3½ cups water, add tomatoes and cook for 2 minutes, uncovered. Drain in a colander. Cool and peel.

• Heat 2 tsp oil in a pan for 30 seconds; add Asafetida, ginger, green chili, and raisins.

• Add peeled tomatoes, ¼ cup water, salt to taste, and sugar; bring to a boil, and simmer for 5 minutes.

• Add black pepper, roasted cumin powder, and mint; mix well. Serve hot.

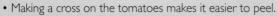

• Making a cross on the tomatoes makes it easier to peel.
• It can also be prepared with large tomatoes. In such case, cut the tomatoes into 1" cubes after peeling.

COCONUT CHUTNEY
Nariyal ki Chutney

INGREDIENTS

1 cup Coconut (*nariyal*), fresh, grated

½ cup Bengal gram (*chana dal*), dehusked, split, roasted

2 tsp Green chilies, chopped

½ tsp Salt

¾-1 cup Water to blend

2 tbsp Cilantro (*dhaniya*) leaves, chopped

For the tempering:

1 tbsp Vegetable oil

½ tsp Bengal gram, dehusked, split

½ tsp Split black gram (*dhuli urad dal*), dehusked

¼ tsp Mustard seeds (*rai*)

2 Dry red chilies (*sookhi lal mirch*)

8 Curry leaves (*kadhi patta*)

METHOD

- Blend coconut, roasted Bengal gram, green chilies, salt, and water to a smooth paste in a food processor. Add cilantro leaves and blend again for 10 seconds.

- Transfer to a bowl and keep aside.

- **For the tempering**, heat 1 tbsp oil in a pan for 30 seconds; add the lentils and cook until light brown. Add mustard seeds, dry red chilies, and curry leaves. Remove and pour over the chutney and serve.

- This chutney is generally served with south Indian snacks such as *idli*, *upma*, etc.
- Coconut chutney is always prepared fresh for authentic flavor.
- Leftover chutney should be refrigerated.
- Roasted Bengal gram is available in grocery stores.

SWEET CHUTNEY
Meethi Chutney

Makes: 1½ cups

INGREDIENTS

1½ cups Jaggery (*gur*), broken into small pieces
2 tbsp Mango powder (*amchur*)
1½ tsp Salt

For masala A:

1 tsp *Garam masala*
(see p. 184)
2 tsp Roasted cumin (*jeera*) powder (see p. 184)
1 tsp Black salt (*kala namak*)

For masala B:

$\frac{1}{8}$ tsp Asafetida (*hing*)
2 tsp Ground coriander (*dhaniya*)
2 tsp Red chili powder

METHOD

- Mix jaggery with 1½ cups water in a pan and cook, on low heat, until it dissolves. Strain and keep aside.

- Mix mango powder in 1½ cups water.

- Mix jaggery water with mango water. Add salt and bring to a boil, simmer for 40 minutes. Remove and cool.

- Dry roast *masala* B ingredients in a pan, until light golden brown. Keep aside.

- Add *masala* A and *masala* B to the cooked jaggery and mango powder mixture and mix well.

- *Meethi* chutney can be stored in the refrigerator for up to a month.
- It can be served with any snack.

JAGGERY FLAVORED MANGO CHUTNEY
Aam ki Launji

Serves: 4-6

INGREDIENTS

1 lb Raw mangoes (*kairi*), peeled, cut into 1" cubes
2 tbsp Jaggery (*gur*), powdered
1 tbsp Vegetable oil
$\frac{1}{8}$ tsp Asafetida (*hing*)
¼ tsp Fenugreek seeds (*methi dana*)
¼ tsp Cumin (*jeera*) seeds
¼ tsp Fennel (*saunf*) seeds
1 tsp Red chili powder
1 tsp Turmeric (*haldi*) powder
1 tsp Ground fennel
½ tsp Salt
¼ cup Water

METHOD

- Heat 1 tbsp oil in a pan for 30 seconds on medium heat; add Asafetida, fenugreek seeds, cumin seeds, and fennel seeds. Add red chili powder, turmeric powder, ground fennel, and cut mangoes; mix well.

- Add salt and ¼ cup water; cook, covered, on low heat, until mangoes are slightly soft. Add jaggery and cook, covered, for 2 minutes on low heat. Remove and serve.

- *Aam ki launji* has a tangy flavor.
- This *chutney* can last in the fridge for up to 15 days.

- All kinds of *paratha* can be enjoyed with this chutney.

FRESH MANGO PICKLE
Aam ka Tazaa Achaar

Serves: 8-10

INGREDIENTS

2 Raw mangoes (*kairi*), cut into medium-sized cubes with skin

2 tsp Mustard seeds (*rai*)

½ tsp Fenugreek seeds (*methi dana*)

4 tsp Ground fennel (*saunf*)

2 tsp Ground coriander (*dhaniya*)

¾ tsp Turmeric (*haldi*) powder

2 tsp Red chili powder

3 tsp Salt

1 tbsp White vinegar (*sirka*)

2 tbsp Mustard (*sarson*) oil

METHOD

- Grind mustard seeds and fenugreek seeds together.

- Mix the ground seeds with fennel powder, coriander powder, turmeric powder, red chili powder, salt, white vinegar, and mustard oil to form a *masala* paste.

- Mix the *masala* paste with mango pieces and set aside for 2 hours. Serve.

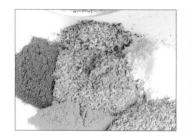

- Refrigerate for later use, but consume within 30 days.

- Mixed *masala* paste can be stored for up to 6 months in the refrigerator.

LEMON FLAVORED GINGER
Nimbu ka Adrak

INGREDIENTS
¾ cup Ginger (*adrak*), peeled,
cut into 1"-long pieces
2 tsp Salt
2 tbsp Lemon (*nimbu*) juice

METHOD
• Mix the cut ginger with
  salt and lemon juice; leave
  aside for 30 minutes at
  room temperature, covered.
  Refrigerate and serve.

• Ginger turns pink in color after left mixed with lemon juice and salt.
• Refrigerate for later use.

TANGY RADISH FLAKES
Mooli ka Kas

Serves: 4-6

INGREDIENTS

1 cup Radish (*mooli*), peeled, grated
2 tsp Salt
1½ tbsp Ginger (*adrak*), peeled, grated
2 tsp Green chilies, chopped
1 tbsp Cilantro (*dhaniya*) leaves, chopped
1 tbsp Lemon (*nimbu*) juice

METHOD

• Mix the grated radish with 1½ tsp salt; leave aside for 2 minutes, squeeze and discard the water.

• Mix squeezed radish with ginger, green chilies, cilantro leaves, ½ tsp salt, and lemon juice. Refrigerate and serve.

• Radish is high in water content. Adding salt and squeezing later improves the texture and prevents the radish from getting watery.

• Normally *mooli ka kas* is served during lunch time.

GREEN CHILI PICKLE
Hari Mirch ka Achaar

Serves: 4-6

INGREDIENTS

¼ lb Green chilies, thick, large, washed, wiped dry, slit vertically, keeping shape intact, seeded
¾ tbsp Salt
½ tbsp Fenugreek seeds (*methi dana*)
1 tbsp Mustard seeds (*rai*)
2 tbsp Ground fennel (*saunf*)
1½ tsp Turmeric (*haldi*) powder
2 tsp Ground coriander (*dhaniya*)
1½ tbsp Lemon (*nimbu*) juice
¼ tsp Asafetida (*hing*)
2 tbsp Mustard (*sarson*) oil
2 tsp White vinegar (*sirka*)

METHOD

- Grind fenugreek seeds and mustard seeds together to a fine powder in a food processor; remove. Mix this powder with ground fennel, turmeric powder, ground coriander, lemon juice, Asafetida, 1 tbsp mustard oil, and white vinegar.

- Stuff each chili evenly with this mixed *masala*.

- Apply 1 tbsp oil on the stuffed chilies and consume after 2 days.

- *Hari mirch ka achaar* should be consumed within 7 days. For extended use, refrigerate to avoid deterioration.

QUICK GREEN CHILI PICKLE
Jhatpat Hari Mirch ka Achaar

Makes: 8-10

INGREDIENTS

4 oz Green chilies, washed, wiped-dry, slit vertically

For the filling: mix and keep aside

4 tsp *Chaat masala*

1 tsp Salt

For the seasoning:

1½ tbsp Mustard (*sarson*) oil

a pinch Asafetida (*hing*)

¼ tsp Fenugreek seeds (*methi dana*)

¼ tsp Cumin (*jeera*) seeds

2 tsp Gram flour (*besan*)

Other Ingredients

1 tsp Ground coriander (dhaniya)

2 tsp Fennel (*saunf*) powder

½ tsp Mango powder (*amchur*)

¼ tsp Salt

METHOD

• Fill each green chili evenly with the filling mixture.

• Heat 1½ tbsp oil in a pan for 30 seconds on medium heat; add Asafetida, fenugreek seeds, cumin seeds, and gram flour; cook for 10 seconds.

• Add stuffed green chilies and mix.

• Add ground coriander, fennel powder, mango powder, and salt; cook on high heat for a minute, stirring constantly. Remove and serve.

• This chili is spicy with a pungent flavor.
• Adding gram flour to this pickle brings out its true flavor.

PICKLED ONIONS
Sirkewale Pyaz

INGREDIENTS

2 Onions, medium-sized, cut
into 1" cubes, layers separated
2 tbsp White / Balsamic vinegar
(*sirka*)
1½ tsp Salt
½ cup Water

METHOD

- Mix the onions with white or balsamic vinegar, salt, and water; leave aside, covered, for an hour. Serve.

- Pearl onions can also be used instead of regular onions.
- Discard water before serving.

- It can be served with any meal.
- Onions turn dark pink when mixed with vinegar.

MANGO MARMALADE
Aam ka Kas

Makes: 2 cups

INGREDIENTS

1 kg Raw mangoes (*kairi*)
3 cups Sugar
2 tbsp Salt
¼ tsp Asafetida (*hing*)
1 tsp *Garam masala*
(see p. 184)

METHOD

• Peel and grate the mangoes.

• Mix the grated mangoes with sugar and salt. Keep covered for 30 minutes.

• Cook on medium heat, stirring occasionally, to one string consistency (see p. 200).

• Turn off the heat, add Asafetida and *garam masala*; mix well. Cool and store in an airtight jar.

• *Aam ka kas* can be stored for up to six months
• This marmalade is served with meals.

• It has a unique sweet and sour flavor.

DESSERTS

SUNRISE PUDDING
Boondi Bake

INGREDIENTS

6 Bread slices
1 cup Gram flour (*besan*)
Clarified butter (*ghee*) for deep-frying
¾ cup Sugar
½ tsp Green cardamom (*choti elaichi*), ground
¼ tsp Saffron (*kesar*)
1½ cups Milk
1¼ cups Heavy cream (see p. 200)
2 tbsp Almonds (*badam*), blanched, chopped (see p. 202)
2 tbsp Pistachios (*pista*), blanched, chopped (see p. 202)

METHOD

- Remove the sides of the bread with a sharp knife, toast them lightly in a toaster, without browning. Keep aside.

- Combine gram flour with ¾ cup water and prepare a semi-thick batter. Heat 1½"-deep clarified butter in a shallow pan; pour the batter through a *boondi* ladle or a slotted spoon and fry until light golden brown. Remove and keep aside.

- Mix the sugar with ¼ cup water in a pan and cook on medium heat, stirring occasionally, to one-string consistency (see p. 200); turn off the heat. Add green cardamom and saffron powder (see p. 203); mix well.

- Add the fried *boondi* to the sugar syrup, mix until well coated; cool. Grind coarsely in a food processor. Keep aside.

- Arrange the bread slices in an 8" square dish, cover with *boondi* and pour milk evenly over it. Bake in the oven at 275°F for 10-15 minutes or until light brown.

- Remove decorate with double whipped cream, almonds, and pistachios. Serve immediately.

- This popular Indian dessert is a melody of crunchy baked *boondi* and chilled cream.

- Indian desserts should always be prepared in clarified butter for better taste.

FRUIT AND CUSTARD PUDDING
Thanda Phalon ka Custard

INGREDIENTS

1 cup Pulp-free orange juice
1 tbsp Agar agar (China grass)
3 tbsp Water
2 tsp Butter
6 Marie biscuit crumbs
(see p. 199)
4 tbsp Custard powder
5 cups Milk
4 tbsp Sugar
4 cups Mixed fruits, chopped
(orange, banana, apples)

METHOD

• Make the jello according to the recipe on p. 201.

• Melt 2 tsp butter in a pan, mix with biscuit crumbs. Remove and press in a 6" shallow serving dish. Leave in the refrigerator for 45 minutes to set.

• Mix the custard powder in ½ cup milk. Set aside.

• Mix the remaining 4½ cups milk with sugar in a pan and bring to a boil on medium heat. Add custard powder mixture and stir constantly to one boil. Turn off the heat, cool, and chill.

• To arrange, remove the chilled biscuit crumb dish from the fridge, spoon the chilled custard over the crumbs, cover with chopped fruits, and top with set jello. Serve chilled.

• Fruit and custard pudding is very popular among teenagers.
• Custard powder should be mixed in room temperature milk, or else it gets lumpy.

• Hot custard can also be served in winter with cakes.
• Set jello can be cut with a sharp knife to any size desired.

INDIAN RICE PUDDING
Chawal ki Kheer

Serves: 4-6

INGREDIENTS

2 tbsp Basmati rice
¼ tsp Saffron (*kesar*)
4 Green cardamom (*choti elaichi*), deseeded
¼ tsp Clarified butter (*ghee*)
7½ cups Milk
4 tbsp Sugar
2 tbsp Almonds (*badam*), blanched, chopped (see p. 202)
2 tbsp Pistachios (*pista*), blanched, chopped (see p. 202)

METHOD

- Wash and soak the rice in plenty of water for 10 minutes; drain. Keep aside.

- Pound saffron and green cardamom together to a fine powder (see p. 203).

- Heat ¼ tsp clarified butter in a heavy-bottom saucepan; add soaked rice and cook for a minute. Add milk and bring to a boil. Reduce heat and cook until the mixture is reduced to third its original consistency, stirring occasionally.

- Add sugar and cook for 10 minutes on low heat. Add cardamom and saffron powder and turn off the heat. Cool and refrigerate the mixture. Serve chilled garnished with almonds and pistachios.

- This is a popular easy-to-make Indian dessert.
- *Kheer* can be served either hot or cold.

- *Kheer* can be made one day in advance and kept in the fridge.
- Blanched and chopped almonds and pistachios add to the flavor.

VERMICELLI PUDDING
Sewai ki Kheer

Serves: 4-6

INGREDIENTS

½ cup Vermicelli (*sewai*)
6 cups Milk
3 Green cardamom (*choti elaichi*), seeded
¼ tsp Saffron (*kesar*)
½ tsp Clarified butter (*ghee*)
2-3 tbsp Sugar
2 tbsp Raisins (*kishmish*)
2 tbsp Pistachios (*pista*), blanched, chopped (see p. 202)

METHOD

- Pound green cardamom and saffron to a powder (see p. 203). Keep aside.

- Heat ½ tsp clarified butter in a shallow pan for 30 seconds; add vermicelli and cook on low heat, stirring constantly, until light golden brown. Add milk and bring to a boil. Reduce heat and simmer for 30 minutes.

- Add sugar and raisins; cook for 5 minutes, turn off the heat.

- Add cardamom and saffron powder; mix. Serve hot or cold garnished with pistachios.

- This is a quick dessert to make on short notice.

- Vermicelli packets are easily available in Indian grocery stores.

SWEET SAFFRON RICE
Meetha Kesari Chawal

Serves: 4-6

INGREDIENTS
2/3 cup Basmati rice
½ tsp Green cardamom (*choti elaichi*), seeded
¼ tsp Saffron (*kesar*)
½ cup Sugar
¼ cup Water
½ cup Almonds (*badam*) blanched (see p. 202), cut lengthwise
2 tbsp Pistachios (*pista*) blanched (see p. 202), cut lengthwise
4 tbsp Clarified butter (*ghee*)
2 Cloves (*laung*)

METHOD
- Wash and soak the rice in plenty of water for 30 minutes, drain. Cook in boiling water until done and strain (see p. 190).

- Pound green cardamom and saffron to a fine powder (see p. 203). Keep aside.

- Mix sugar and water in a pan and cook on low heat to two-string consistency (see p. 200). Turn off the heat, add ¾ of both cut almonds and pistachios. Add powdered saffron and cardamom and cooked rice to the syrup; mix and leave covered for 2 hours. Stir occasionally.

- Heat 4 tbsp clarified butter in a pan for 30 seconds; add cloves and when it begins to change color remove and add this seasoning to the rice mixture. Mix gently.

- Serve hot or cold, garnished with remaining almonds and pistachios.

- Boiled rice added to sugar syrup leaves water initially, but soaks up after 2 hours.

- *Meetha kesari chawal* is a delicacy and is generally served along with meals.

CARROT PUDDING
Gajar ka Halwa

Serves: 4-6

INGREDIENTS

2 lb Carrots (*gajar*), peeled, grated
5 cups Milk
1¼ cups Sugar
¼ lb Whole milk fudge (*khoya*) (see p. 201)
4 tbsp Clarified butter (*ghee*)
1 tsp Ground green cardamom (*choti elaichi*)
½ cup Cashew nuts (*kaju*), chopped
½ cup Almonds (*badam*), blanched, chopped (see p. 202)
¼ cup Pistachios (*pista*), blanched, chopped (see p. 202)

METHOD

- Combine the grated carrot with milk in a large pan and cook on medium heat, stirring occasionally, until the milk evaporates.

- Add sugar and cook on low heat until the mixture is semi-thick, turning frequently.

- Add grated whole milk fudge and cook on low heat for 10 minutes, turning frequently.

- Add clarified butter and cook on low heat, turning constantly for 15 minutes. Turn off the heat, add ground cardamom and chopped cashew nuts; mix well.

- Serve hot, garnished with almonds and pistachios.

- Discard the hard center portion of the carrots while grating.
- Carrot pudding can be stored in the fridge for up to a week.

- Red carrots can also be used instead of the orange ones. In fact, red carrots needs less sugar as they are sweeter in taste.

HOT SEMOLINA PUDDING
Suji Halwa

INGREDIENTS
¾ cup Semolina (*suji*)
6 Green cardamom (*choti elaichi*), seeded
¼ tsp Saffron (*kesar*) strands
¾ cup Sugar
1¾ cup Water
5 tbsp Clarified butter (*ghee*)
2 tbsp Gram flour (*besan*)
¼ cup Almonds (*badam*), blanched, chopped (see p. 202)
2 tbsp Pistachios (*pista*), blanched, chopped (see p. 202)

METHOD
- Pound green cardamom and saffron into a fine powder (see p. 203). Keep aside.

- Prepare sugar syrup by mixing sugar and water in a pan and boiling the mixture, on low heat, until the sugar dissolves. Keep aside.

- Heat 4 tbsp clarified butter in a shallow pan for a minute; add semolina and gram flour and fry on low heat, until light golden brown, stirring frequently.

- Add sugar syrup and stir constantly, on low heat, until the mixture becomes semi-thick.

- Add cardamom and saffron powder, mix. Add the remaining 1 tbsp clarified butter and mix. Serve hot garnished with almonds and pistachios.

- Water should be added to fried semolina 30 minutes before serving, otherwise the pudding becomes too thick.

- Adding 1 tbsp clarified butter later improves the texture of the pudding.

SAFFRON PISTACHIO DELIGHT
Kesar Pista Kulfi

INGREDIENTS

10 cups Milk
5 tbsp Sugar
¼ tsp Saffron (*kesar*)
8 Green cardamom (*choti elaichi*), seeded
2 tbsp Pistachios (*pista*), blanched, chopped (see p. 202)
8 *Kulfi* molds

METHOD

- Pound saffron and green cardamom to a fine powder (see p. 203).

- Heat the milk in a shallow pan and cook on medium heat until reduced to ¼ its original consistency, stirring occasionally.

- Add sugar and cook for 2 minutes. Turn off the heat. Add saffron-cardamom powder to the condensed hot milk; mix well and cool.

- Mix the milk mixture with 1½ tbsp pistachios and blend in a mixer for 10 seconds. Pour into the *kulfi* molds, sprinkle remaining pistachios on top, cover the molds with the lid and freeze for 10-12 hours or until set.

- De-mold set *kulfi* with a sharp knife. Remove to a plate, cut into slices and serve.

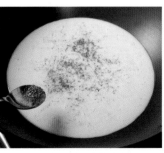

- Use whole milk for better taste.
- It can also be made with skimmed milk for weight watchers.

- For easy unmolding, wash the frozen *kulfi* molds under running water.

SWEET COCONUT SQUARES
Nariyal Burfi

Serves: 8-10

INGREDIENTS

16 oz Coconut (*nariyal*), fresh, grated
2¼ cups Sugar
7 oz Whole milk fudge (*khoya*), grated (see p. 201)
1 tbsp Rose water (*gulab jal*)
Vegetarian Silver leaves (*varq*) for decoration
2 tbsp Almonds (*badam*), blanched, chopped (see p. 202)
2 tbsp Pistachios (*pista*), blanched, chopped (see p. 202)

METHOD

- Mix grated coconut with sugar and leave for 30 minutes in a shallow pan. Cook on medium heat, mixing constantly, until a sugar coating is seen on the surface, while turning.

- Add grated whole milk fudge and rose water; mix well.

- Transfer to a greased tray (8" × 4") and press down immediately. Leave to set for 4 hours.

- Decorate with silver leaves, almonds, and pistachios, and cut into square pieces. Serve.

- Select medium-ripe coconuts and scrape south-Indian style.
- Silver leaves are mainly used for decoration, and do not contribute to the taste.

- For the sugar coating to form it takes 20-30 minutes.
- This Indian sweet can be kept for up to a week. It is an ideal preparation for Holi, Diwali, and other festivals.

SWEET DIAMONDS
Shakkar Pare

INGREDIENTS

2 cups All-purpose flour (*maida*)

3 tbsp Clarified butter (*ghee*) melted

Lukewarm water to make the dough

2½ cups Clarified butter for deep-frying

1 cup Sugar

$\frac{1}{3}$ cup Water

METHOD

- Sieve the flour, add 3 tbsp melted ghee and knead to prepare a hard dough with lukewarm water. Keep aside covered for 10 minutes.

- Divide the dough into 2 equal balls, roll each ball into ¼"-thick disc and cut into ½" cubes.

- Heat 2½ cups clarified butter in a shallow frying pan until medium-hot; add the cubes and deep-fry until light golden brown. Remove and cool.

- Prepare sugar syrup with sugar and water to one-string consistency (see p. 200); turn off the heat.

- Add fried cubes into the sugar syrup and keep mixing until sugar coating is formed on the cubes. Remove, cool, and store.

- This Indian sweet is particularly made on the festival of colors, Holi.
- It can be stored for up to 20 days in a cool, dry place.

SWEET DUMPLINGS LACED IN SYRUP
Gulab Jamun

INGREDIENTS
½ lb Whole milk fudge (*khoya*)
(see p. 201)
2 oz Cottage cheese (*paneer*)
¼ cup All-purpose flour (*maida*)
2¼ cups Sugar
2¼ cups Water
2½ cups Clarified butter (*ghee*)
for deep-frying

METHOD
- Prepare sugar syrup by mixing sugar and water in a pan and boiling the mixture, on low heat, cook until the sugar dissolves, strain. Keep aside.

- Mash whole milk fudge and cottage cheese to a smooth paste separately, with a rolling stone. Mix the two pastes with flour and prepare a soft dough.

- Divide the dough equally into 20-25 portions and shape them into round balls.

- Heat 2½ cups clarified butter in a shallow pan on low heat; add 15 balls at a time, and watch until they float, increase heat to high and cook until golden brown, turning frequently and gently with the spatula.

- Remove, add them to the sugar syrup and leave for an hour. Reheat with sugar syrup and serve hot.

- *Khoya* also called *khawa* or *mawa* is a common ingredient in many traditional Indian sweets. When milk is slowly evaporated under heat, it eventually becomes a solid mass which is called *khoya*.

- *Gulab jamun* is a popular Indian dessert
- *Gulab jamun* can last for up to 10-15 days in the fridge.
- It can also be stuffed with chopped almonds and pistachios.

COOKING PROCESSES

BAKING POTATOES AND SWEET POTATOES

• Apply oil to the sweet potatoes.

• Apply oil to the potatoes.

• Bake at 400°F for 20-30 minutes or until soft.

• Bake at 400°F for 20-30 minutes or until soft.

• Cool and peel.

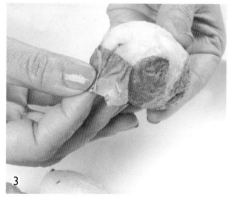

• Cool and peel.

BAKING TIP

• Applying oil to the potatoes / sweet potatoes helps to remove the skin easily.

PRESSURE COOKING POTATOES / GREEN BANANAS / RAW MANGOES

- Place raw potatoes in the pressure cooker, add enough water to cover, cook to one whistle. Simmer for 4 minutes.

- Place green bananas in the pressure cooker, add enough water to cover, cook to one whistle.

- Place raw mangoes in the pressure cooker, add enough water to cover, cook to one whistle.

- Cool and drain.

- Simmer for 4 minutes. Cool and drain.

- Simmer for 4 minutes. Cool and drain.

- Peel and use as per recipe.

- Peel or mash and use as per recipe.

PREPARING SPICE MIXES

CHANA MASALA

- Mix together 2 tbsp coriander seeds, 2 tsp cumin seeds, 5 cloves, 1" cinnamon stick, 2 seeded black cardamom, 8 black peppercorns, and 4 dry red chilies.

SPICE TIP
- These spice mixes can be stored for up to two weeks.

- Dry roast all the spices on low heat, until light golden brown.
- Cool and grind coarsely.

ROASTED CUMIN POWDER

- Roast 2 tbsp cumin seeds in a pan, on low heat, stirring frequently, until golden brown.

GARAM MASALA

- Mix together 2 tbsp black peppercorns, 8 seeded black cardamom, and 2 tsp cloves.

- Store in an airtight jar.

- Cool and grind coarsely.

- Grind to a powder.

Peanut Powder

- Heat 2 tbsp oil in a pan until medium-hot; add ½ cup peanuts and fry until light brown. Remove and cool.

2

- Remove the skin with fingers.

3

- Coarsely powder in a mortar and pestle, if recipe requires.

Roasting Semolina

- Dry roast semolina in a shallow pan for 5 minutes on low heat; remove.

Roasting Vermicelli

- Heat the clarified butter (as per recipe) in a pan for 30 seconds.

- Sauté vermicelli on low heat, stirring constantly, until light golden brown.

Magori

Magoris are sun-dried split green gram dumplings. They are made by soaking and grinding split green gram, shaping them into small balls, and drying in the sun.

- Deep-fry *magoris* in medium-hot oil until light golden brown.

2

- Crush slightly if recipe requires (this releases its flavor).

COOKING WITH TOMATOES

• Seeding tomatoes

1

• Cut tomato into quarters vertically, remove the seeds with a sharp knife.

2

• Cut as required in the recipe.

• Roasting tomatoes

1

• Hold the head of the tomato with a fork over direct heat, turning all over, until the skin shrinks.

2

• Cool and remove the skin.

• Grating tomatoes

1

• Cut tomato into half, vertically.

2

• Grate from the cut side down until the tomato skin.

TOMATO GRAVY / TOMATO YOGURT GRAVY

TIP
• The quantity of ingredients to be used as per recipe.

1

• Heat the oil in a pan; add asafetida, cumin seeds.

2

• Add turmeric powder and red chili powder; mix.

- Making liquidized tomato

- Cut tomato into 8 pieces.

- Blend to a smooth paste.

ONION-TOMATO GRAVY

- Heat the oil; add bay leaves, cinnamon, cloves.

- Add grated onion, and ginger-garlic paste; fry until golden brown.

- Add red chili powder and turmeric powder; mix.

- Add liquidized tomato and fry until oil separates.

- Add liquidized tomato, ginger, chili paste. Cook until oil separates.

- To make tomato-yogurt gravy, add beaten yogurt to the cooked tomato gravy.

- Cook until oil separates. Add water.

WORKING WITH COTTAGE CHEESE

- **Making plain cottage cheese** *(paneer)*

- Bring 5 cups milk to a boil in a pan, on medium-heat, turn off heat. Add 1-2 tbsp lemon juice, gradually, stir until milk curdles.

- Fold cloth over cottage cheese, molding, into a square shape.

- Wait for 2 minutes.

- Place a light weight over the cottage cheese for 20 minutes. Alternatively, place in a cottage cheese maker and cover with the lid for 20 minutes.

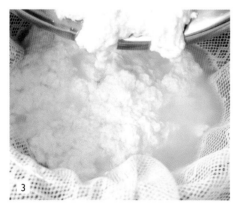

- Drain in a muslin cloth.

- Cut off any uneven edges. Use immediately or refrigerate for later use.

COTTAGE CHEESE TIP
- 5 cups milk makes 5 oz of cottage cheese.

• Making *masala* cottage cheese

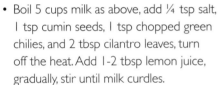

• Boil 5 cups milk as above, add ¼ tsp salt, 1 tsp cumin seeds, 1 tsp chopped green chilies, and 2 tbsp cilantro leaves, turn off the heat. Add 1-2 tbsp lemon juice, gradually, stir until milk curdles.

• Wait for 2 minutes. Drain.

• Place in a cottage cheese maker and cover with the lid for 20 minutes.

• Cut off any uneven edges. Use immediately or refrigerate for later use.

• Sautéing cottage cheese

• Heat 2 tsp oil in a non-stick pan for 30 seconds; add cottage cheese and sauté on both sides, on medium heat, until light golden brown.

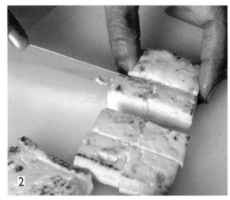

• Remove and cut into cubes.

BOILING RICE

MAKING DOUGH

I

- Wash and soak I cup rice in 4 cups water for 30 minutes. Drain.

I

- Sieve flour. Add all the ingredients (such as oil, clarified butter, yogurt, milk) given in the recipe except water.

2

- Boil 6½ cups water. Add soaked rice, bring to a boil and cook, covered, on low heat until the rice is soft.

2

- Dough may be soft, normal, or hard. Adjust the quantity of water for a soft or hard dough, as required in the recipe.

3

- Remove, drain in a colander, and transfer to a serving dish.

3

- Picture shows normal dough.

RICE TIP

- To check if the rice is cooked press with the index finger for softness.

DOUGH TIP

- Dough can be kneaded with hand or in a food processor.
- For normal dough, add 1½ cups water for 4 cups flour and knead well.

MAKING FRESH COOKING PASTES

Ginger Paste

- Take 2 tsp of chopped ginger.

- Hand pound chopped ginger to a fine paste, keep aside. Use as required.

Garlic Paste

- Take 8 garlic cloves.

- Hand pound chopped garlic cloves to a fine paste, keep aside. Use as required.

Chili Paste

- Take 2 tsp of chopped green chilies.

- Hand pound chopped green chilies to a fine paste, keep aside. Use as required.

PRESSURE COOKING LEGUMES

- **Pressure cooking yellow lentil** (*arhar dal*)

- Soak 1 cup in 3 cups water for 30 minutes; drain. Put in a pressure cooker.

- Add 1½ cups water.

- Add ¾ tsp salt and ½ tsp turmeric powder. Pressure cook to one whistle and simmer for 4 minutes.
- Open the lid when the pressure drops.

- **Pressure cooking horse gram** (*kala chana*)

- Soak 1 cup horse gram in 5 cups water for 8 hours; drain. Put in a pressure cooker.

- Pressure cook with 1¼ cups water and ¼ tsp salt to one whistle, simmer for 20 minutes. Open the lid when the pressure drops.

LENTIL TIP
- Make sure that the pressure drops before removing the lid to ensure that the legumes are fully cooked.

- **Pressure cooking chickpeas** (*kabuli chana*)

- Soak 1 cup chickpeas in 5 cups water for 8 hours; drain. Put in a pressure cooker.

- Add 2½ cups water.

- Add ¼ tsp salt and cook to one whistle; simmer for 30 minutes. Open the lid when the pressure drops.

- **Pressure cooking kidney beans** (*rajmah*)

- Soak ¾ cup beans in 4 cups water for 4 hours; drain.

- Put the beans in a pressure cooker and add 2 cups water.

- Add ¼ tsp turmeric powder and ¼ tsp salt; cook to one whistle and simmer for 30 minutes. Open the lid when the pressure drops.

- **Pressure cooking black-eyed peas** (*lobhia*)

- Soak ¾ cup peas in 4 cups water for 4 hours; drain. Put in a pressure cooker..

- Add 2 cups water.

- Add ¼ tsp turmeric powder and ¼ tsp salt; cook to one whistle and simmer for 5 minutes. Open the lid when the pressure drops.

TEMPERING LENTILS

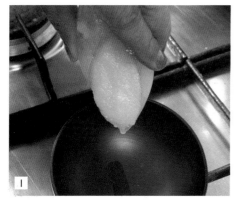

- Heat the clarified butter in a pan for 30 seconds.

- Add asafetida.

• Variation with curry leaves

- Heat the clarified butter in a pan for 30 seconds.

- Add cumin seeds and cook until the seeds start spluttering.

- Add mustard seeds and curry leaves.

- Remove from heat and add dry red chilies (if recipes requires) and red chili powder or ground black pepper.

- Add red chili powder.

COOKING WITH VEGETABLES

• Blanching Beans and Carrots

• Boil 5 cups water, add 1 cup beans and carrots each.

• Blanching of Bean Sprouts

• Boil 4 cups water and add 2 cups bean sprouts.

• Blanch for 2 minutes.

• Cook for 2 minutes, uncovered.

TEMPERING TIP
• Remove the pan from heat to prevent chili powder from burning as this will spoil the flavor of the dish.
• Follow quantity and ingredients in the order given in the recipe.

BLANCHING TIP
• Blanching, also called par-boiling, is lightly cooking raw vegetables for varying amounts of time in boiling water.

• Drain in a colander.

• Drain and use as per recipe.

COOKING WITH VEGETABLES

• **Spinach**

• Heat the pan; add 1 lb chopped spinach and ¼ tsp sugar.

• Cook covered for 2 minutes.

• Remove and use as per recipe.

• **Fenugreek leaves**

• Heat the pan; add ½ lb chopped fenugreek leaves and ¼ tsp sugar; cover and cook for 1 minute.

• Remove and use as per recipe.

Corn

- Heat 2 tsp oil in a pan for 30 seconds; add 2 cups corn and cook for 2 minutes, on high heat, stirring frequently.

- **Peas**

- Heat ½ tbsp oil in a pan; add 2 cups peas and ¼ tsp salt. Cook, covered, on low heat until soft.

- Remove and use as per recipe.

- Remove and use as per recipe.

TIP
- Adding ¼ tsp sugar while cooking spinach and fenugreek helps to retain the green color.

WORKING WITH YOGURT

Setting Yogurt

- Heat 5 cups milk until lukewarm.

2

- Add ½ tsp yogurt culture.

3

- Mix lukewarm milk and yogurt culture thoroughly.

4

- Leave to set in a warm place for 3-6 hours. Refrigerate.

1

- **Making hung yogurt for salad dressing:** place 2 cups yogurt in a sieve or in a muslin cloth for 2-3 hours.

2

- **Making yogurt for *raita* and *dahi pakodi*:** place 2 cups yogurt (as per recipe) in a sieve for 30 minutes.

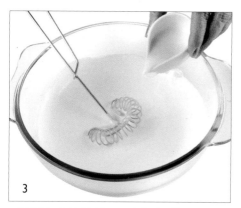

3

- Whisk. Add ¼-½ cup chilled milk to get a soft, creamy consistency.

WHILE MAKING DESSERTS

Biscuit crumbs

1

- Place 6 tea biscuits in a bag.

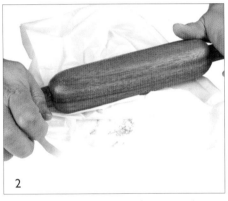
2

- Press with rolling pin to form crumbs.

Bread Squeezing

1

- Dip 2-4 slices of bread in 2½ cups water.

3

- Add 2 tsp melted butter, mix. Place and press in a serving dish. Refrigerate for 45 minutes until firm. Follow the recipe.

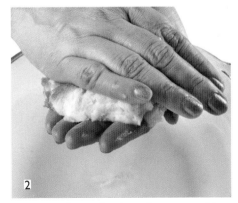
2

- Remove immediately and squeeze with your palms.

YOGURT TIP

- Always set yogurt using lukewarm milk (100°-110°F). Putting culture into hot milk spoils the texture and taste of the yogurt.
- Yogurt sets faster in summer while it takes longer in winter.
- Once set, refrigerate to prevent it from getting sour.

HUNG YOGURT TIP

- Milk is normally added to get the right consistency and flavor.
- Hanging yogurt removes excess water and milk gives it a fresh taste.

WHILE MAKING DESSERTS

Whipped Cream

I

- Mix 1¼ cups chilled heavy cream with ¼ cup chilled milk.

2

- Add 2 tbsp confectioners' sugar and 2 tsp rose water. Blend in a food processor until semi-thick.

3

- Use as required in the recipe and consume within 24 hours.

Sugar Syrup

I

- Mix ¾ cup sugar with ¼ cup water in a shallow pan and bring to a boil, on low heat, stirring occasionally.

2

- To check the string, place a drop of syrup on a plate.

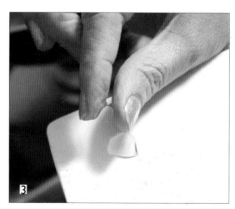

3

- Check between thumb and index finger.

WHIPPED CREAM TIPS
- Use chilled heavy cream and milk to avoid curdling.
- Over blending may also lead to separation of butter from cream-milk mixture.
- For variation, use ½ tsp vanilla essence instead of rose water.

CUSTARD TIPS
- Custard powder should be mixed with room temperature milk otherwise it tends to get lumpy.

SUGAR SYRUP TIPS
- **One-string consistency**: a thin string is formed when testing the sugar syrup between thumb and index finger.
- **Two-string consistency**: when testing the sugar syrup between thumb and index finger, two strings are formed.

KHOYA TIPS
- After milk is reduced to about one fourth the amount, stir constantly to avoid sticking to the bottom of the pan, otherwise it may have a burned smell.

Custard

- Take 5 cups milk. Mix 4 tbsp custard powder in ½ cup milk.

- Boil the remaining 4½ cups milk with 4 tbsp sugar.

- Pour the custard mixture to the boiling milk, stirring constantly.

Khoya (Whole-milk Fudge)

6¼ cups Whole milk, unsweetened

Method:

Bring milk to a boil in a non-stick pan. Cook unti it reduces to a solid, soft mass over moderate heat, stirring frequently. Let cool to room temperature.

- Turn off the heat after one boil. Remove, keep aside to cool. Serve chilled.

Jello Making

- Mix 2 cups of pulp-free orange juice and 2 tbsps Agar agar (China Grass) flakes.

- Cook on low heat and bring to a boil, stirring constantly.

- Let it set in the fridge until firm. Remove with a knife or spoon. Serve chilled.

PEELING AND CHOPPING NUTS

1

• Soak ½ cup almonds in 1½ cups water for 8 hours, covered.

1

• Soak ½ cup pistachios in 1½ cups water for 8 hours, covered.

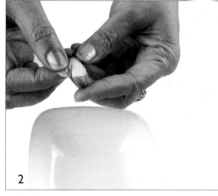

2

• Peel.

2

• Peel.

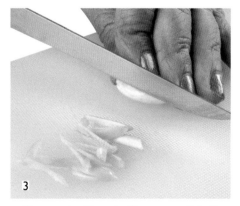

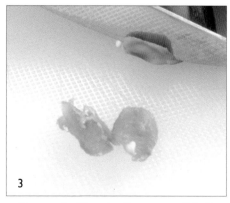

3

• Chop and refrigerate. Consume within 2 days.

3

• Chop and refrigerate. Consume within 2 days.

TIP

• Peeled almonds and pistachios taste better than unpeeled in Indian desserts.

MAKING SAFFRON CARDAMOM POWDER

1

- Seed 8 cardamom pods.

2

- Add ¼ tsp saffron strands.

3

- Pound both to a fine powder.

4

- Use quantities as indicated in each recipe.
- Saffron and cardamom can also be pounded individually.
- It can also be stored in the refrigerator for 15 days.

MEAL MENUS

1

DRINK, SALAD & APPETIZER

Minty Lemonade
Hara Bhara Nimbu Pani   25
Salad Medley with Jaggery Dressing
Mila Jula Salaad   37
Cottage Cheese Fritters
Paneer Pakodi   44

MAIN COURSE

Lentil Dumplings and Spinach in Yogurt Sauce
Magori Palak ki Kadi   77
Curried Kidney Beans
Rajmah   79
Potatoes and Bell Pepper
Aloo Shimla Mirch   82
Corn a la Cilantro
Dhaniyawale Makai ke Dane   96

RICE & BREADS

Cumin Pilaf
Jeera Pulao   124
Spicy Indian Bread
Masala Paratha   136
Plain Indian Bread
Sada Roti   137

ACCOMPANIMENT

Tempered Liquid Buttermilk
Tarka Mattha   152

DESSERT

Carrot Pudding
Gajar ka Halwa   173

2

DRINKS, SALADS & APPETIZER

Tomato Cucumber Melody
Tamatar Khira Lajawab   26
Tomato and Cottage Cheese Salad
Tamatar aur Masala Paneer Salaad   39
Sago Cutlets
Sabu Dana Vada   56

MAIN COURSE

Dumplings in Spicy Yogurt Sauce
Kadi Pakodi   74
Fenugreek Flavored Lentil
Urad Chana aur Methi Dal   80
Healthy Leafy Vegetables
Hara Saag   102
Mixed Vegetables with Cottage Cheese
Sabz Paneer   106

RICE & BREADS

Plain Rice
Crisp Indian Bread
Khasta Roti   139
Plain Indian Bread
Sada Roti   137

ACCOMPANIMENT

Plain Yogurt

DESSERT

Fruit and Custard Pudding
Thanda Phalon ka Custard   169

3

DRINK, SALAD & APPETIZER

Iced Tea
Sharbati Chai   21
Corn Salad
Makai Salaad   34
Crispy Baby Corn
Chhote Karare Bhutte   43

MAIN COURSE

Roasted Spiced Eggplant
Baingan Bharta   90
Stuffed Green Chilies
Bharwa Mirchi   98
Curried Colocasia
Rasedar Arvi   110
Spicy Chickpeas
Chana Masala   112

RICE

Fenugreek Flavored Cottage Cheese Pilaf
Methi Paneer Pulao   126

ACCOMPANIMENT

Spinach Flavored Yogurt
Palak Raita   153

DESSERT

Vermicelli Pudding
Sewai ki Kheer   171

4

DRINK, SALAD & APPETIZER

Tender Coconut Cooler
Daab Shikanji 24

Chickpea Salad
Kabuli Chana Salaad 33

Floret Fritters
Gobi Pakodi 45

MAIN COURSE

Spiced Green Bananas in Yogurt Curry
Kele ki Kadi 73

Beans with Baby Corn
Beans aur Chhote Bhutte 94

Curried Lotus Stem
Sookhi Kamal Kakri 103

Cottage Cheese with Peas in Gravy
Mattar Paneer 117

BREAD

Flaky Mint Bread
Lachchedar Paratha 134

Plain Indian Bread
Sada Roti 137

ACCOMPANIMENT

Fruity Yogurt
Anar aur Ananas Raita 147

DESSERT

Sunrise Pudding
Boondi Bake 168

5

DRINK, SALAD & STARTER

Spiced Yogurt Drink
Mattha 20

Sweet Potato and Bean Sprout Salad
Chatpata Shakarkandi Salaad 38

Stuffed Chili Fritters
Bharwa Mirchi ki Pakodi 47

MAIN COURSE

Stuffed Okra
Bharwa Bhindi 93

Hot Potato Curry
Aloo ka Jhol 108

Lentil Dumplings with Fenugreek and Peas
Methi Magori Mattar 118

RICE & BREAD

Mixed Vegetable Pilaf
Sabz Pulao 127

Carom Spiced Puffs
Namak Ajwain ki Puri 142

ACCOMPANIMENT

Lentil Dumplings in Creamy Yogurt
Dahi Pakodi 149

DESSERT

Indian Rice Pudding
Chawal ki Kheer 170

6

DRINK, SALAD & STARTER

Mango Mocktail
Aam Panna 22

Potato and Pickled Onion Salad
Aloo Pyaz, Sirkewale 36

Potato Fritters
Aloo Pakodi 46

MAIN COURSE

Spicy Green Lentil
Sabut Moong ki Dal 81

Cauliflower and Potatoes
Aloo Gobi 88

Bottle Gourd Dumplings in Tomato Gravy
Lauki Kofta 114

Bitter Sweet Creamy Peas
Methi Malai Mattar 119

RICE & BREAD

Corn Pilaf
Bhutte ka Pulao 123

Plain Indian Bread
Sada Roti 137

Fenugreek Bread
Besan Methi Roti 138

ACCOMPANIMENT

Yogurt with Lentil Pearls
Boondi Raita 148

DESSERT

Saffron Pistachio Delight
Kesar Pista Kulfi 175

COMMON ACCOMPANIMENTS

Green Chutney
Hari Chutney 154

Jaggery Flavored Mango Chutney
Aam ki Launji 158

Lemon Flavored Ginger
Nimbu ka Adrak 160

Tangy Radish Flakes
Mooli ka Kas 161

Green Chili Pickle
Hari Mirch ka Achaar 162

SNACK MENUS

1

Spicy Indian Puffs
Pani Puri   64
Spicy Chaat Bowls
Chaat Katori   66
Spicy Potato Patties
Chatpati Aloo Tikki   57
Lentil Dumplings in Creamy Yogurt
Dahi Pakodi   149
Green Chutney
Hari Chutney   154
Sweet Chutney
Meethi Chutney   157

2

Lentil Pancakes
Moong Dal Cheela   51
Savory Rice Flakes
Poha   60
Sago Cutlets
Sabu Dana Vada   56
Mushroom Cheese Toast
Khumbi Toast   54
Green Chutney
Hari Chutney   154
Sweet Chutney
Meethi Chutney   157

3

Toasted Garden Sandwiches
Hara Bhara Toast   55
Potato Fritters
Aloo Pakodi   46
Spicy Semolina
Rawa Upma   62
Dry Green Lentil
Sookhi Moong Dal   50
Green Chutney
Hari Chutney   154
Sweet Chutney
Meethi Chutney   157

4

Vegetable Vermicelli
Sabzdar Sewai   63
Savory Lentil Cakes
Chatpata Dhokla   52
Corn on Toast
Karare Makai Pav   42
Savory Semolina Cakes
Rawa Idli   61
Coconut Chutney
Nariyal ki Chutney   156
Green Chutney
Hari Chutney   154

GLOSSARY OF FOOD AND COOKING TERMS

Bake To cook in the oven by dry heat.

Batter A mixture of flour, liquid, and sometimes other ingredients of a thin, creamy consistency.

Blend To mix together thoroughly two or more ingredients.

Coat To cover food that is to be deep-fried with batter.

Curdle To separate milk into yogurt and whey by acid or excessive heat.

Deep-fry Sufficient oil is used to cover the food completely. The pan used must be deep enough to be only half full of oil before the food is added.

Fry To cook in hot oil.

Garnish An edible decoration added to a dish to improve its appearance.

Grease To coat the surface of a dish or tin with fat to prevent food from sticking to it.

Grind To reduce hard food such as legumes, lentils, spices, and so forth, to a fine or coarse paste in a grinder or blender.

Knead To work a dough by hand or machine until smooth.

Purée To press food through a fine sieve or blend it in a blender or food processor to a smooth, thick mixture.

Sauté To cook in an open pan in hot, shallow fat, tossing the food to prevent it from sticking.

Seasoning Salt, pepper, spices, herbs, and so forth, added to give depth of flavor.

Shallow-fry A small quantity of fat is used, in a shallow pan. The food must be turned halfway through to cook both sides.

Simmer To boil gently on low heat.

Steam To cook food in steam. Generally food to be steamed is put in a perforated container which is placed above a pan of boiling water. The food should not come in contact with the water.

Stir-fry To fry rapidly while stirring and tossing.

Stock Liquid produced when vegetables are simmered in water with herbs and spices for several hours.

Syrup A concentrated solution of sugar in water.

Temper To fry spices and flavorings in hot oil or clarified butter, and to pour this over the main preparation.

Whisk To beat rapidly and introduce air into a light mixture; such as yogurt.

THE STATE OF HUMAN DEVELOPMENT

"The test of our progress is not whether we add more to the abundance of those who have much; it is whether we provide enough for those who have too little."

US President Franklin D. Roosevelt, second inaugural address, 1937 [1]

Human development is about freedom. It is about building human capabilities—the range of things that people can do, and what they can be. Individual freedoms and rights matter a great deal, but people are restricted in what they can do with that freedom if they are poor, ill, illiterate, discriminated against, threatened by violent conflict or denied a political voice. That is why the "larger freedom" proclaimed in the UN Charter is at the heart of human

development. And that is why progress towards the MDGs provides a litmus test for progress in human development. There is more to human development than the MDGs themselves—and many of the MDG targets reflect a modest level of ambition. But failure on the MDGs would represent a grave setback.

The most basic capabilities for human development are leading a long and healthy life, being educated and having adequate resources

Progress and setbacks in human development

The first section of this chapter is a brief overview of the progress and setbacks in human development over the past decade and a half. It highlights the great reversal in human development inflicted on many countries by HIV/AIDS, and the slowdown in progress on child mortality. Uneven progress across countries and regions has been accompanied by a divergence in human development in some key areas, with inequalities widening. The second section of the chapter turns to the MDGs. The limited—and slowing—advances in human development achieved over the past decade have a direct bearing on prospects for achieving the MDGs. Average incomes in developing countries have been growing far more strongly since 1990. Yet this income growth has not put the world on track for the MDGs—most of which will be missed in most countries. Part of the problem is that growth has been unequally distributed between and within countries. The deeper problem is that increased wealth is not being converted into human development at the rate required to bring the MDGs within reach. Our country-level data projections set out one possible set of outcomes that will follow if the world remains on the business-as-usual trajectory that the UN Secretary-General has warned against.

- The MDG target for reducing child mortality will be missed, with the margin equivalent to more than 4.4 million avoidable deaths in 2015. Over the next 10 years the cumulative gap between the target and the current trend adds more than 41 million children who will die before their fifth birthday from the most readily curable of all diseases—poverty. This is an outcome that is difficult to square with the Millennium Declaration's pledge to protect the world's children.

- The gap between the MDG target for halving poverty and projected outcomes is equivalent to an additional 380 million people in developing countries living on less than $1 a day by 2015.

- The MDG target of universal primary education will be missed on current trends, with 47 million children in developing countries still out of school in 2015.

Statistics such as these should be treated with caution. Projections based on past trends provide insights into one set of possible outcomes. They do not define the inevitable. As the financial market dictum puts it, past performance is not a guide to future outcomes. In the case of the MDGs, that is unambiguously good news. There is still time to get back on track—but time is running out. As the UN Secretary-General has said: "The MDGs can be met by 2015—but only if all involved break with business as usual and dramatically accelerate and scale up action now."[4]

e MDG target for
g child mortality
missed, with the
gin equivalent to
e than 4.4 million
le deaths in 2015

1 The state of human deve

"We have a collective
responsibility to uphold
the principles of human
dignity, equality and equity
at the global level. As
leaders we have a duty
therefore to all the world's
people, especially the most
vulnerable and, in particular,
the children of the world, to
whom the future belongs."

Millennium Declaration, 2000[2]

Sixty years ago the UN Charter pledged to free future g
of war, to protect fundamental human rights and "to p
better standards of life in larger freedom". At the start
world's governments renewed that pledge. The Millenr
in 2000, sets out a bold vision for "larger freedom" in the
vision holds out the promise of a new pattern of globa
foundations of greater equity, social justice and respect fc
lennium Development Goals (MDGs), a set of time-bou
for reducing extreme poverty and extending universal ri
benchmarks for measuring progress. More fundamentall
aspirations of the global human community in a period of

This year marks the start of the 10-year count-
down to the 2015 target date for achieving the
MDGs. Today, the world has the financial,
technological and human resources to make a
decisive breakthrough in human development.
But if current trends continue, the MDGs will
be missed by a wide margin. Instead of seizing
the moment, the world's governments are stum-
bling towards a heavily sign-posted and easily
avoidable human development failure—a failure with profound implications not just for the
world's poor but for global peace, prosperity
and security.

Fifteen years after the launch of the first
Human Development Report, this year's Report
starts by looking at the state of human development. Writing in that first report, Mahbub
ul Haq looked forward to a decade of rapid
advance: "The 1990s", he wrote, "are shaping
up as the decade for human development, for
rarely has there been such a consensus on the
real objectives of development strategies."[3]
Since those words were written a great deal has
been achieved. Much of the developing world

has experienced ra
living standards. N
globalization. Yet
vances fall short of
Development Repo
what was possible.

Viewed from th
is a growing danger
the past 10—will g
decade of accelerated
as a decade of lost op
deavour and failed i
This year marks a cro
community can eithe
tinue on its current h
or it can change direc
policies needed to turr
lennium Declaration ii

The consequences
current path should r
Using country-level trer
human cost gaps in 2015
and predicted outcomes
tinue. Among the headli